Dance of
Leadership

ROBIN DENISE JOHNSON, Ph.D.

Editor: Lorna Adams
Copy Editor: Kay Huxford
Text Graphics and photographs courtesy of Charlene M. Sieg

To purchase copies call QP Distribution at 888-281-5170 (toll free)
or contact sales@novuspublishing.com

Printed in the United States of America

ISBN 0-9755143-4-2

First Edition

Novus Publishing, LLC

Please visit our website at http://www.novuspublishing.com

CONTENTS

ACKNOWLEDGEMENTS

My heartfelt gratitude goes to the many people who have informed my thinking, encouraged my leadership and supported my efforts in writing this book. Thank you Gabrielle Roth—we've never met but I've loved and used your Endless Wave CD to sweat my prayers for many years. Susan Golant helped me focus on this as a book concept and frame the entire project. Heartfelt thanks, Susan. Thank you to my many dance teacher colleagues – especially Aziza Said who encourages all her students to dance their unique dance, Gloria Paternostro who makes ballroom dancing fun, and Ellisa Kyriacou who models the power of dancing for life – each helped me experience the dance and envision the lessons found in the dance of leadership. Thank you, Alex Horniman and Jim Clawson, for being willing to explore and teach the lessons of leadership in unconventional ways. Thank you, Pat Heim, for encouraging me to write from my heartfelt experience. Thank you, David Porter, for asking me to join you in teaching a wonderful group of leaders through the UCLA Leadership Suite and Laurie Dowling and the folks in EEP for your unwavering support. I have deep respectful appreciation for all the lessons I've learned about leading and dancing from my students, executive education participants and coaching clients. Thank you all. And many thanks from the heart for the images from Charlene Sieg who provided the graphics used in this book. Charlene was the first to articulate how I used lessons from dance in teaching my classes - opening my eyes to dance as a metaphor for leadership - and she regularly demonstrates the power of stillness for bringing out the best in me and others.

I dance! I didn't always know I was a dancer. I've danced most of my life in one way or another. Sure, I was dancing, but I didn't really see myself as *a dancer*. As far as I was concerned, dancers were "professionals"—people who were "trained", who "performed" on stage, and who, if they were lucky, made a living from their "artistry". In short, dancers were recognized, and they were far more skilled than I was. Me? I just danced.

The same notion may apply to you and your thoughts about yourself as a leader. Most likely, you're out there leading everyday, but you may not see yourself as *a leader*. You've probably thought, "Leaders are gifted, special, professionally-trained people who have positions at the top of the organization, not ordinary people like me." It's easy to miss your own leadership, especially when the majority of the leaders we hear about, see in our media, or encounter in our organizations seem to be extraordinary people who have somehow been anointed to lead. These individuals are overwhelmingly characterized as "special" in some way.

I am writing this book to help you (and our society) change that mindset. In fact, my message is: Leading is Natural. Leading is Life. Leadership is a Dance. It doesn't take the big shot head of a mucky-muck corporation to understand leading or the pointy headed intellectual to be able to write about it. We can all do it—mucky-mucks and schmucks, intellectuals and couch potatoes, homemakers and outdoorsy types—we can all lead from being ourselves doing our lives with the intention of making a positive difference in our world. When we live from that place of meaningful intention, leading is as easy and as natural as dancing.

This book is for you if...
- You aspire to leadership to make a positive difference, right where you are, in your authentic way.
- You are in a position of exercising influence but not in a position of authority. (This applies to 'middle' managers anywhere in the world.)
- You appreciate management/leadership as an art, not just as a lifeless-do-it-by-the-numbers-only activity.
- You are ready for an easy-to-relate-to and non-threatening image of effective leadership.
- You are ready to see your self, your style, and your interactions as significant too.

DANCE OF LEADERSHIP

Chapter 1
INTRODUCTION

WHY THE *DANCE* OF LEADERSHIP?

Dance is one of my core passions—all sorts of dance: oriental dance, ballroom, social tango, tribal dance, afro-Caribbean dance, jazz, and modern dance—it doesn't matter. And because of this, I have searched for ways to use the lessons I've learned from dance in the leadership classes I teach at top business schools to students and executives. People take my classes because they aspire to be leaders in business. Executives attend leadership programs because they want to become and be seen as effective leaders. Sometimes they have been promoted to leadership positions but they seek to beef up their inner sense of leading—their skills and their confidence.

My class sessions are favorites because I always blend theoretical knowledge with experiential learning—mind and body—and I encourage every participant to get to know and then lead from his or her center. I do the same with my executive coaching clients. Some of my clients do not yet believe they fit popular notions of "A LEADER"—they are not yet at the very top of their organizations, or they may have started a company and be at the top, but they may not be white heterosexual alpha (ultra-confident, powerful, dominant) males. My students, executive education participants, and clients come in all kinds of racio-ethnic and gender packages. What they have in common is that they are committed, talented, caring people who are seeking to contribute in meaningful ways to their organizations while maintaining a fulfilling, balanced, whole life. They respond well to the dance

1

metaphor because it is easy to experience and to see the link between art and discipline in dance—and the similar requirement to understand leadership as both art and discipline resonates with them.

Dance provides a physical metaphor for leading and following and teaches us many lessons. In fact, when you read this book, you will learn:

- Your personal dance/leadership style—how to know it, how to develop it and when to use it effectively.
- That leadership is more than position or power-over others; leadership is a relationship between followers and leaders.
- That leaders come in all shapes, sizes, levels, colors, and genders.
- How to listen to both your inner voice and the outer rhythm—so that your movements-actions are timely and appropriate to your specific leadership situation.
- How the frame-boundaries you set support you and your followers and make the entire process of leading-following more secure for everyone.
- Why resistance to your leadership is helpful and why followers must provide it in order for change to occur. Resistance is not rigidity, and knowing the difference is important.
- That leading in high performing teams means sharing authority when all members are capable of performing their tasks well, and every team member trusts the process and each other.

In the *Dance of Leadership*, I will explore with you leadership lessons I learned from dancing, and provide examples as we go along.

Awakening the Leader in You

My leadership coaching practice is filled with people who seek out my advice because someone has told them I can help them articulate, understand, and reach some professional goal. My approach is holistic. Goals are rarely just professional, though people often come in presenting a "career issue." And more often than not, I find these individuals are unacknowledged leaders—that is, they lead others but they have only a vague idea that they're doing so. Unfortunately, this lack of self-awareness and intentionality can sometimes get them into hot water and can even thwart their continued success. They may misinterpret or misdiagnose what's going on and overlook opportunities to resolve problems. As a result, similar difficulties keep recurring.

Take the situation Marge found herself in. Nearly a decade before she engaged me as a coach, she had written the original grant to obtain funding for a not-for-profit program within a sprawling social service agency. As a result of her good work, this particular program had grown over the years, receiving larger and larger grants and requiring the effort of more and more people. From being one person managing herself and a small program, Marge was now leading seventeen people and juggling a 2 million dollar budget. But somehow, she had missed the fact that along the way, she'd become a "leader" within her large agency.

Indeed, when she came to see me, she brought into our discussion what she thought was a fairly superficial misunderstanding she was having with some of the people working with her. At an awards banquet, she had recognized Chloe for her extraordinary community service. But other members of her program became upset at this, feeling Marge favored Chloe over them. There was behind-the-scenes grumbling and rebellion in the air. Although Marge believed this to be a trivial problem, the incident helped surface a disconnect between her view of herself—an individual working with many others at a large social service agency that served their community—and her coworkers'

3

perception of her—their leader who signaled who and what was important through her recognition award.

Once Marge had a more accurate perception of herself and her role, once she started to see herself as a leader *within* (although not necessarily at the top of) her organization, she was able to think more clearly about the impact of her decisions and behaviors on it and on the people with whom she worked. Marge was involved in the dance of leadership but was totally unaware of it. Now she knows it, has gotten a few lessons to improve her performance, and is finally enjoying the dance to boot.

Leading is often a self-fulfilling prophecy. People who don't see themselves as leaders don't behave as leaders. They don't take responsibility; they don't change situations they could change; they don't encourage others when they could. All of this reduces their organization's effectiveness and sense of community, reduces their feelings of personal efficacy and empowerment, reduces their personal life-meaning and satisfaction, reduces their opportunities for growth and spiritual fulfillment, and reduces their sense of having accomplished what they've been put on this earth to do (what Buddhists call "right action"). That's a huge organizational and personal price to pay for a simple misperception. Knowing yourself as a leader, a person able to make a significant difference right where you are while using whatever sources of power you have in your own style, will increase your organizational effectiveness while empowering you and others.

What Makes Us Leaders?

Much of what has been written about leadership assumes that a leader is a person in a position of recognized authority who therefore has the right to lead—the Top Dog, Numero Uno, the Big Cheese—the CEO, the president, the boss. In this country, we're taught to strive for that top position. What's that expression on tshirts, "Only the lead dog gets the good view"? Although there are many autobiographies outlining the successes of such industry giants as Lee Iococca, Bill Gates, Jack Welch or even former New York mayor Rudy Guilliani, search as you may, I dare you to find a book entitled: *How I Became A Great Follower*.

Once we identify what we consider to be "true" leaders, we then spend lots of time and energy trying to decide:

- Why are they the right person for the job? What are their leadership traits and do we have them?
- How can we become more like them? What do we need to learn in order to develop leadership characteristics ourselves?
- How do we recognize situations that would suit our aspirations as wannabe leaders? How can we position ourselves to demonstrate our abilities?

Underneath all this is the assumption that leaders are special people, above us, whose gifts others recognize. In fact, most people only see leadership as *position*—the person at the pinnacle of the organizational pyramid is designated "it." As a consequence, we've granted these anointed ones the right to influence and make decisions for us in particular situations.

With this view in mind, it would not be surprising that many of us abdicate our own responsibilities as leaders as well as followers. Many times, just like Marge, our own leadership potential and leading behaviors are invisible to us because we see the leader as that gifted, special person at the top of the heap. But, we most likely say to ourselves, we're neither gifted (not yet, anyway, but we're always striving to become so), nor are we at the top (because if we were, we'd see ourselves as leaders). Many entrepreneurs can at least say "I'm at the top" but if they are at the top of small businesses, they quickly discover they have little power and influence over their clients and team members since everyone is spending most of their time struggling to survive. The position might say leader, but it doesn't feel like leader in terms of power. Add to this the observation that most so-called leaders in our society are white and male, and so may not resemble many of us demographically. And, if you are a white male who leads but doesn't see himself as extraordinary, or a woman, or a person of color of either gender, extraordinary or not, you may find that the popular models of leaders don't apply to you, and so you discount your own leadership potential.

To change that mind-set, we all need a new definition of leadership. Power has many sources. When we talk about leadership, I particularly want to separate positional power (the authority inherent in the top-dog position) from personal sources of power such as character, traits, and charisma. Using authority—your power-over people—and your control over resources, will often get you coerced or co-opted performance. That can be OK, and even appropriate at certain times. The other sources of power leaders can use—charisma, relationships, involvement, respectful listening, expertise, character, and trustworthiness—all ways to have power-with, are more likely to get you committed performance. These traits and skills help leaders build high quality committed teams, get people to pull in the same direction, resolve conflicts, and develop the people who work with them.

So, let's redefine leadership as something more than position and "leaders" as more than simply "those at the top," so more of us can recognize ourselves as leaders and lead effectively. In fact, I like to think of leaders as individuals who *cause or influence others to make a positive difference toward the achievement of a shared goal.* You don't need to be the top banana to make a positive difference. You can lead from the middle, from within your organization, and achieve a whole lot of success doing so. (And in the process, you will also become more understanding of the challenges your positional leaders face as they shoulder our collective expectations of "leader perfection.") And even if you

6

are at the top—you can use many of the other sources of power to influence others, not just positional authority.

In fact, in actual practice, far more of us are leading everyday from within our organizations than we realize. Take, for example, Donna's situation. Her boss and a supplier were in conflict. Six months earlier, the supplier had promised a product. As it turned out, the supplier couldn't deliver what was contracted for but actually came up with a better product at the same cost. Nevertheless, Donna's boss, Bill, was angry about the breach. He went on and on about how the supplier had broken its promise. Initially, Donna saw herself as being "in the middle"—that is, she had made the initial order and was now caught in the crossfire between the supplier and her irate boss. After we discussed this situation, she came to see that she could take a leadership role in this dispute. In fact, she was able to mediate between the two parties and helped them resolve their differences. She got them both to focus on the *business need* rather than the broken promise—a win-win for all. Her company was now able to use the enhanced product and the supplier was off the hook for its breach. Donna used her 'pull' influence style to mediate the dispute and make a positive difference.

Lianna was also able to act as a leader from within her organization. She was assigned to be team leader for what she called "a bunch of cowboys"—individualistic employees who rarely worked together, hoarded information from each other, and not surprisingly, were fairly unproductive. She was the nominal or positional team leader, but in fact, had no team to lead—just an assortment of individuals, each bent on having their autonomy. Her first challenge, then, was to lasso the cowboys into a working herd. She knew that she couldn't do this alone, so she took the initiative to approach her boss for money to hire a team-building consultant. With the aid of this consultant, Lianna created a *real* team that she now leads. Lianna's ability to create a real team and keep it focused on a shared, larger goal made a positive difference.

Larry was also able to make a positive difference. His organization had given him a budget of $14.00 a person for an upcoming holiday party. "How cheap!" his subordinates grumbled. Not wanting to succumb to their negative energy, Larry found a way to redirect their resistance into more productive channels. He asked the most vociferous complainers to join the party-planning committee. It was their task to find a way to celebrate the holidays within the constraints of the tight budget. Charged with that mission, the complainers used their creativity to devise a solution that built on their company's other holiday activities. And a good time was had by all. Larry's ability to channel resistant energy towards productive goals made a positive difference.

Raj had an "extraordinarily competent" subordinate who wasn't always confident about her abilities. Raj saw Jacqui's potential, however, and suggested that she make a lateral move within the organization that would help her develop new skills thereby positioning her for promotion in the future. It was a risk for both of them that paid off handsomely. Jacqui learned the new job quickly and well, others recognized her competence, and she was promoted. And Raj was thrilled and proud of having seen and directed Jacqui's energy into a wider sphere. Raj's willingness to mentor a gifted subordinate made a positive difference.

In all four cases we saw each person decide—set an intention—to make a positive difference. They did it in different ways—conflict management, team building, channeling resistance, and mentoring—and all four responses are ways of leading that use more than positional power. Each person responded, not just reacted, but thoughtfully responded, to the needs of their situation with the skills they had to make a difference. And each person responded authentically.

In order to lead from within, you must be authentic. You need to know what making a positive difference means to you.

Once you recognize this, once you start to see yourself leading in particular areas of your life, you begin to open to the lessons and responsibilities of leading in life. Take, for instance, Jaime's situation. He had just been promoted from the rank-and-file into management in a big company in Texas. As it turned out, his organization was simultaneously embarking on a major new diversity initiative with plans for marketing campaigns, diversity training, "multicultural days," and so on. Lots of hoopla but, unfortunately, no real substance, or as they say in Texas, "Big hat, no cattle!"

Jaime felt strongly that diversity would work better if the efforts were more substantive—if the program demonstrated how different kinds of people could actually work productively together—rather than this flashy program that he called "smoke and mirrors." Although he was brand new in his role as a manager, he suggested to the diversity organizers that the change efforts start with a pilot program: a diverse team that would focus on learning and developing productive behaviors together. This learning could then be disseminated throughout the company after the pilot period ended. Jaime's grassroots philosophy was "Show me, don't tell me." This was far more convincing to the rank-and-file, demonstrating a stronger commitment to diversity than the glitzier, PR-driven approach. Consequently, it was far more effective. Jaime knew that people would respond positively to a change when it was genuine rather than superficial. He acted from his authentic self—he led from *within himself* as well as from *within his company*—and made a positive difference for everyone.

WHAT MAKES LEADERS?

Are Marge, Donna, Lianna, Larry, Raj, and Jaime leaders? Are they gifted, special, professionally trained, extraordinary individuals or just everyday people like you and me? Let's examine, for a moment, the three questions people ask most often about leaders:

- What are leaders' <u>born</u> traits that make them successful?
- What did they learn and experience that <u>made</u> them leaders?
- How and why were they <u>called</u> to lead?

These questions form the backbone of this book, leadership research and leadership practice. Essentially they ask us to consider a larger question: *What makes leaders?* Are they born, made, or do they emerge from situations that call them forth? This question represents the major directions academic leadership research has taken over the years. But rather than bore you with all the theoretical details, I'd like to answer that basic question with an analogy from dance.

As an African-American, I've frequently heard the "positive" stereotype that Black people have natural rhythm. Indeed, I have a strong sense of rhythm myself. Dance feels natural for me. But I've also noticed in my family and in many others within the African American community that music, especially the heartbeat pulse of the drum, is played constantly. People growing up in these communities hear both the heartbeats of their mothers and the rhythm of the drum from the time they are in the womb. I remember how I tried to move with that beat when I was young, but I was no more successful at on-beat movement than many other first-timers. I was, however, *motivated* to do so and had many *opportunities* to learn since this was an important aspect of my environment.

My teachers showed me how to hear and move with the beat. They bounced me up and down in time with the music. They encouraged me when I got it right and corrected me when I was "off". I put in the effort and kept trying until my dancing-on-the-beat skill became as "natural" as it is now.

So when people ask about leadership—whether leaders are born, made, or called by the situation—I think of the lessons I learned from the dance, and it's clear that it's not an either/or proposition. Leaders are born (they have certain innate traits and talents that generate energy and motivation), made (willing to learn and develop their skills) *and* they respond to the situational call.

So what are the broader implications of this?

First of all, it's important not to get caught up in thinking that there is just one path to leading. We lead when we're lucky. Luck is when opportunity meets preparation. Your business is to prepare:
- To know yourself, your inborn traits.
- To develop your talents and skills.
- To set your intention to respond when called.

"Opportunity", as this saying goes, "is God's business." You just need to respond when God / the universe / your situation / life calls you to lead.

Secondly, when you are being authentically yourself and are willing to make a positive difference, you will be called upon in situations where your unique talents and gifts are just what are needed. That's what happened to Jaime when his company began to unroll its new diversity program. Leaders are born with gifts, develop those gifts *and* respond/share those gifts with others when the circumstances arise. So, leaders are born, made and called!

Because this is such an important concept, I've organized the *Dance of Leadership* around these three interrelated ways of becoming a leader. One of the first challenges a solo dancer has is to recognize and dance in his or her authentic style. We are all born with certain traits, propensities and/or preferences that become our signature style. Living from our style, being authentic, is the first step to being an effective leader. Leadership literature is full of exhortations to know your style, move to your inner drummer, and develop techniques that allow you to express yourself.

And this brings up the question of finding a mentor. We will often send a student to the teacher rather than paying attention to which teacher the student actually needs. Indeed, it is far more helpful to allow our talents and style to guide us in seeking a teacher who will help us develop what is already present within us—not the other way around. Similarly, we often try to learn about leading without first deciding what talent-skills-gifts-inclinations we have that will make a positive difference, AND without setting our intention about that difference. We then try to lead according to someone else's notion of leadership, which is like trying to dance in someone else's style. And then we're surprised when we are less effective than we'd like to be!

So the first step to leading is in determining and articulating your personal style. Performing artist, dancer and teacher Gabrielle Roth developed a movement program describing five basic dance rhythms: flowing, staccato, chaos, lyrical, and stillness. Through listening to and moving with each rhythm we learn which type(s) of movement and music are natural for us, and which do not move us, literally.

HOW THIS BOOK IS ORGANIZED

In Chapter 2 of this book I provide a short questionnaire that will provide you with some insight into a pattern of rhythms that may resonate with you. I suggest you complete the questionnaire prior to reading about the five styles and that you refine your assessment of your stylistic preference as you read more about each of the five rhythms in subsequent chapters. You will also read brief summaries of key aspects of each of the five rhythms. In Chapters 3 to 7, I describe each one of the five styles in more detail with biographical examples of people using that style. The biographical cases replace the music and kinesthetic exercises we use in Dance of Leadership workshops to help people identify and understand their style. In chapter 8, I discuss the born? made? called? issue, provide developmental activities for each style, and link each style to situations likely to call/use that style effectively.

The second section of the book starts with Chapter 9 where we will explore the relationship between leaders and followers. Again, dance provides a wonderful metaphor for exploring relational leading, particularly the importance of a frame-boundaries to secure and support the leader-follower relationship, the specific roles-expectations for leaders and followers, and the use of follower resistance as an effective lever for change. The analects of Confucius provide us with some additional insights in the leader-follower relationship.

Chapter 10 takes on team leadership and we learn lessons from tribal dance. I found it affirming to note that what we learn from tribal dance and what I learned from research into what makes empowered teams, especially diverse teams, work well were mutually supported ideas—that team leadership is a function of appropriate empowerment, real team-spirit (especially task and emotional interdependence), and understanding how the leading functions can, indeed must, be shared by members based on competence and situation. Chapter 11 concludes the book by summarizing the key Dance of Leadership lessons.

REFERENCES

CHAPTER 1

Roth, G. (1997). *Sweat your Prayers: The Five Rhythms of the Soul*. Tarcher Putnam.

Client Examples: All client examples are provided by real people whose names have been changed for confidentiality reasons.

Chapter 2
YOUR LEADERSHIP-DANCE STYLE

B efore I describe the five rhythmic styles, please use the self-assessment tool on the next few pages. This is a questionnaire with imagery that appeals to the different rhythmic preferences. I designed this tool to help you decide which rhythm(s) appeals to you on a intuitive level before your head takes over telling you which leadership you ought to have. I have found that participants in my workshops often have a preconceived notion about which leadership style is best, *in general*, rather than an openness to exploring-developing the style that truly resonates-moves them. All of the approaches and rhythms used in this book describe leadership styles that can be effective. There is no best style. So relax. Be willing to believe that there are no accidents, that you have been created to resonate to exactly the style that will be easiest for you to develop, and most appropriate for you to use. Discovering and respecting your style is truly sacred work. Do not worry if you respond-resonate to more than one rhythm. We are all unique and will have a style 'pattern'—a blend of styles often with really strong positive resonance to one or two rhythms, strong negative resonance to one or two rhythms, and the others in between. The most important thing is to listen to your *own* heart, to *your* inner voice, and how they respond to and/or are moved by certain words-pictures-images.

FIVE STYLES QUESTIONNAIRE

Please note your response to the words and the images they conjure, listed below. If a word-image evokes positive energy for you, please give it a 10. If the word-image really turns you off, give it a 0. You may give the words-images any rating between 10 and 0. Put your rating in the shaded box on the same line as the word in the list. For instance, place your rating for "Roller Coaster" in the column marked "B".

(Shaded rating cells are indicated with ▓)

Metaphorical Item	A	B	C	D	E
Roller Coaster		▓			
Kite moving through sky	▓				
Song of a thrush				▓	
The Desert			▓		
Waving wheat	▓				
Flamenco					▓
Swinging				▓	
Weaving	▓				
Niagara Falls		▓			
Confetti				▓	
Fly fishing	▓				
Juggling				▓	
Woodpecker					▓
A single leaf falling from a maple tree	▓				
Rocks			▓		
Sushi Chef					▓
Monkeys		▓			
Mobiles				▓	
Sleeping cat			▓		
Fireworks					▓
Silence			▓		
Snowflakes				▓	
Silk velvet	▓				
Surfing		▓			
Shape shifting				▓	

Metaphorical Item	A	B	C	D	E
Mime			▓		
Metronome					▓
Hula dancing	▓				
Zero			▓		
Dreams		▓			
Kung Fu – Karate – Kickboxing					▓
Boiling water		▓			
Owl			▓		
Sailing	▓				
Fantasy Fiction		▓			
Tap dancing					▓
Improvisational jazz				▓	
Turtle			▓		
Popcorn popping		▓			
Rap Music					▓
Library			▓		
Cloud shadow moving across landscape	▓				
Champagne				▓	
Deep sea diving		▓			
Linearity - Cubism					▓
Avalanche		▓			
Spring season				▓	
Robot					▓
Eagle in flight	▓				
Orchids			▓		
	A	B	C	D	E
SUBTOTALS - THIS PAGE					
SUBTOTALS - PREVIOUS PAGE					
TOTALS					

Now sum up your responses in each of the columns and place that sum on the bottom line "TOTALS". You should have a score between 0 and 100 for each column.

Select the column with the highest total. That is where you have the greatest metaphorical resonance.

- If your highest score is in column A, you have your highest resonance with **FLOWING.**
- If your highest score is in column B, you have your highest resonance with **CHAOS.**
- If your highest score is in column C, you have your highest resonance with **STILLNESS.**
- If your highest score is in column D, you have your highest resonance with **LYRICAL.**
- If your highest score is in column E, you have your highest resonance with **STACCATO.**

If your highest scores are tied with two columns, you resonate to both those styles at the cogno-emotional level.

Also note where you have your lowest resonance.

Remember! This is just to give you some indication of how the different rhythms evoke stronger, more positive energy for you, strong negative energy for you, or moderate energy for you at an intuitive, metaphorical level. This is not a test. You cannot fail it. It is simply designed to provide you with some insight.

A: FLOWING

 The flowing rhythm has a "fluid, circular, continuous motion" that embodies constantly shifting sound and movement like a meandering river or an undulating snake, sinuous, able to change direction when needed but generally progressing slowly, yet inexorably, toward a goal. The hallmark of the flowing rhythm is contiguity—each movement being connected to the next in a clear and obvious way. All movement is grounded, earthy, clear. Metaphorically, flowing is about knowing your core self, and moving from that place—grounded in your values. It's knowing yourself in connection to others, to the earth, and to all-that-is.

The Flowing leader takes things one step at a time—seeing how each movement informs and causes the next. These leaders take their time to assess where the movement is in their organization. They think through their decisions and behaviors and move their organizations slowly, yet inevitably towards certain objectives. These leaders are careful to avoid blocking the flow, knowing the power required to stop movement is much greater than the power needed to channel it into desired directions. Their goal is to guide the energy of their organizations to move in ways consistent with the organizing purpose. Movement is visible, extraverted—yet one has the sense that the energy has a force below it that keeps it moving through designated channels no matter what. They move to their inner drummer, focused on their purpose, activity, or goal. Others are often attracted to that sense of enacted purpose and follow them, want to support them, be like them—thus they are leading because their behavior demonstrates the power of tapping into and moving from a sense of shared values and purpose. In the *Magic of Conflict*, Thomas Crum demonstrates the power of aikido—flowing—to manage conflict situations. Mihaly Csikszentmihalyi shows us how the flow can support major creative endeavors.

Other words/metaphors associated with flowing include Argentine Tango, Tai Chi, Ice Skating, the French language, Lomi-Lomi Hawaiian massage, active meditation, calligraphy, or desert dunes.

Motto: Just do it!

Architecturally, flowing looks like the TWA terminal at JFK Airport in New York City.

Flowing-style leaders include Mother Teresa, Michael Jordon, Mary Magdalene, and Cleopatra.

Flowing style art-artist might be *Starry Night* by Van Gogh.

Developmental books for the Flowing leadership style:
The Tao of Leadership by John Heider, et al
The Magic of Conflict by Aikido Master Thomas Crum
Flow: The Psychology of Optimal Experience by Mihaly Csikszentmihalyi

B: CHAOS

 A person resonating to the chaos dance rhythm is comfortable with ambiguity, letting the movement itself control the direction the body takes, knowing that in some situations the body is smarter than the brain. The body and music blend in ways that maximize efficiency. In music, externalized chaos is the polyphonic rhythms of African drums, or internalized in the arrhythmic Arabic taksim—music that seems to be without a clear beat or form to follow yet still propels you to express it.

Chaos implies out of control. The word chaos actually means "empty space" or abyss in Greek. Metaphorically, chaos, the abyss, is the place where contraries meet, mix and dissolve- where opposites meet and clash, unleashing force-energy. It is the gateway to the intuitive mind-body-heart in that part of us that knows our destiny, our purpose, our contribution, our presents (presence), our Self. Chaos tends to get a bad rap in our culture since we seem to want to understand and control most aspects of our lives.

Chaos style leaders know they do not have control, do not have all the answers, cannot save everyone, maybe not even themselves—but on some deeper level they believe in people, they believe in their purpose (even a divine purpose), and they have a deep trust in the Universe-God-Spirit-Divine Organizing principles. Chaos leaders often take a degree of pleasure in smashing the boxes and boundaries many of us hide in so that we feel safe and in control. They show us how the categories we live with may be comfortable at times, but way too tight if we really want to grow and/or solve our more complex problems. The Chaos leader lives-thinks out of the box, and encourages followers to do likewise. Chaos leaders are typically interested in a wide-range of subjects, bringing insights from unrelated areas to bear on problems in particular areas. They are often known to have a

21

quirky sense of humor, to be playful, or at least not to take themselves (or others) too seriously—a characteristic that helps them maintain optimism and some sense of proportion in the face of what might otherwise seem to be overwhelming odds. Chaos leaders are often called upon to provide guidance in times of crisis.

Other words/metaphors associated with chaos include intuition, boiling water, tornados, a junkyard, white water, Greenwich Village in NYC in summer, Mexico City, Cairo.

Motto: "Bust-think out of the box!"

Architecturally, chaos looks like a Frank Gehry building such as the Stata Center at MIT, the Bilbao Museum in Spain or the Disney Concert Hall in Los Angeles.

Chaos style leaders include Bayard Rustin, Bill Clinton, Albert Einstein, and Alexander the Great.

Chaos style art-artists might be a Jackson Pollack painting, and comedians such as Lucille Ball, Jerry Lewis, and Margaret Cho.

Developmental books for the chaos leadership style include:
Leadership and the New Science by Magaret Wheatley.
Thriving on Chaos by Tom Peters

C: STILLNESS

 The essential stillness rhythm would be silence. Stillness in dance may often look like no movement. The energy of stillness is focused on the inner dance where each movement rises from the ocean of being. Other words associated with stillness rhythm include jelly fish, a cloistered convent, the shadow, a cracked mask, Kali Ma, Buddha, a coiled snake, breath meditation—insight meditation. If chaos energy is the surf, stillness is the stone in the water causing it to ripple outward.

Metaphorically, stillness is a deep understanding of the in and the out, the light and the shadow, the head and the heart—all opposites actually contained in unity. The rhythmic energy flow is bounded, directed inward, grounded, and expressed only with intense focus, compassion and detachment.

Leaders who resonate to stillness know how to use silence, how to listen to both the inner and outer voice, how to role model the behavior they want others to emulate, and provide information that helps followers to listen to the guide within and move from following that guidance. Stillness leaders seem to be evident and effective in situations that call for values/belief changes. There is something about their ability to tap into our deeper, shared desires that allows them to get below the surface disagreements and bring our places of shared value to light. Stillness leaders know that organizations consist with reciprocity—the taking in and giving out—with employees, suppliers, customers and community. This reciprocity is to replace their understanding that us vs. them is usually dysfunctional when what you are seeking is a shared goal. Because stillness works with light and shadow, seeing them as aspects of the same energy, Stillness leaders might guide us to and through those parts of ourselves we are most likely to ignore or deny. Many of the Stillness leaders help us see not just our own personal shadows and the consequences of rejecting-projecting that

23

onto individual others—but also to look at the collective-rejected-projected shadow that blocks many more enlightened human efforts to create social equity.

Motto: "Be the change you wish to see in the world."

Architecturally, stillness looks like the Acropolis in Athens.
Georgia O'Keefe's intense still life paintings invoke stillness energy. Stillness style characters might include Yoda from Star Wars. Stillness style leaders include Gandhi, and many of those individuals and leaders influenced by his non-violent civil disobedience as a way to obtain social change—Rosa Parks, the Dalai Lama, Cesar Chavez & Dolores Huerta, Aung San Suu Kyi. and Thich Nhat Hanh—plus all the people who sit, walk, and protest with them using non-violent non-cooperation.

Developmental books for the Stillness leadership style:
The Tao of Personal Leadership by Diane Dreher.
Loving What Is by Byron Katie.

D: LYRICAL

 Lyrical rhythm dancing is seen in the twirling, swirling, airy, light-on-your-toes, reach-for-the-sky elegance associated with ballet. This style is deceptive because it looks far easier than it is. Its beauty emerges from the illusion of lightness and grace. Yet creating the impression that one is not limited by gravity requires incredible strength and balance. Other words that evoke the lyrical rhythm include rope skipping, the acrobatic flight of a raven, Balinese dancers, and the character Alice in the "Alice in Wonderland" story. A lyrical image is that of a duck floating serenely on top of the water, with its feet moving at hyper speed beneath its smoothly floating body.

Metaphorically, the lyrical rhythm re-presents how things are not quite what they seem. Things shift, change, look different depending on perspective—like if you were looking at the duck from above or below the water. Lyrical rhythm is about knowing things are always in process, becoming, changing—and that our so-called fixed reality is an illusion.

As a leadership style, Lyrical tends to be more introverted and involving—you might call it more of a "pull" style if you were to contrast it with the more assertive "push" style of Staccato. The person using the Lyrical style is likely to encourage, engage, inquire, and empathize with others, drawing them out of their shells and/or into the Lyrical leader's orbit. Often these people exercise influence behind the scenes—for which they are sometimes acknowledged, sometimes not. Lyrical leadership shape shifting may look like a person who is able to improvise, think well on their feet, and adapt to new information and opportunities quickly. Lyrical leaders multitask.

The Lyrical style can be effective in situations where you must exercise influence to accomplish tasks but you do not have overt power or authority to get things done—for instance, in the classic middle manager situation where you have responsibilities without sufficient authority to accomplish tasks through-with subordinates. It can also be effective in situations where you are able and willing to work through relationship networks, and/or to improvise quickly to take advantage of opportunities to move the shared agenda forward.

Motto: "Adapt. It's about survival of the fittest."

Architecturally, lyrical looks like Horyu-Ji Temple in Nara Japan.

Lyrical style leader role models might include Princess Diana, Hopi Spider Grandmother and R. Sargent Shriver.

Lyrical style art-artists might include Salvador Dali, J.R.R. Tolkien, Matisse cutouts, CJ Lewis's Alice in Wonderland character, and the Zorro /Robin Hood character.

Developmental reading for the Lyrical leadership style:
Invisible Work: The Disappearing of Relational Practice at Work from the Simmons College Center for Gender in Organizations by Joyce Fletcher, and anything about Emotional Intelligence by Daniel Goleman and his colleagues.

E: STACCATO

 Roth describes the staccato rhythm as "short, sharp, percussive—stops and starts," bursts of energy moving in various directions. A classic example of staccato movement from dance would be flamenco—the stamping, dramatic dance of Spanish gypsies. Staccato is dancing with your bones, creating all kinds of angles and edges like geometry in motion. Lines erupt out of curves, articulating our separateness, creating walls or breaking them down.

Metaphorically, staccato is about getting in touch with your energy, your passion, and expressing that passionate energy to others, while projecting your self into the outside world. Staccato is about doing, not just being; taking action, not just thinking about it. It is directing the flow of energy into clear-cut lines.

As a leadership style, Staccato is a very extraverted "push" style. Staccato leaders assert, direct, coerce, and tell folks what needs to be done. They break rules, take risks, experiment, challenge the status quo, go for the gold, take action—in short they do! Some Staccato style leaders love dramatic flair with their actions; they come in, shake things up, and get everyone energized and moving. Direction of movement is not always as important as taking some action, doing something! The Staccato style may also be clear about drawing in the lines, the boundaries, setting the goals, protecting their key people—while still pushing folks to do what needs to be done. For many of us, staccato is 'the' leadership style leaders should have—its masculine command-control aspects are familiar in our general assumptions of how leaders lead. Staccato leaders know they are making a difference—they intend to and they do. Many entrepreneurs seem to use this style.

The Staccato leadership style also seems to be very effective in situations that call for quick, clear, surgical responses—periods of crisis or emergency situations.

Other words/metaphors associated with the staccato rhythm include Kodo drums, slamming doors, jackhammers, a pounding heart, the Cha-Cha-Cha, a stapler, machine gun fire, lightning, the German language.

Motto: "Ready, fire, aim!"

Architecturally, staccato looks like the Washington Monument in DC or Frank Lloyd Wright's Falling Water home.

Staccato style leaders include (Neutron) Jack Welch, Madame CJ Walker, and Elizabeth Vargas.

Staccato style art-artists include Picasso's cubism, Mick Jagger on stage, Michael Jackson dancing, the 1812 Overture.

Developmental books for the Staccato Leadership Style include:
Straight from the Gut by Jack Welch
Sun Tzu's *Art of War*.

THE 5 STYLES IN NATURE

STACCATO   STILLNESS   FLOW   LYRICAL   CHAOS

  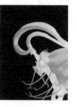 

Nature is a never-ending dance
Of light and shadow
Apparent edges which suggest solid form,
Earth, water, sky
And yet, each part
Touches the next, and the next
Until finally, one
Cannot find the beginning
The middle
Or the end
Of the dance.

—Char Sieg

REFERENCES

Chapter 2

Crum, T. F. (1987). *The Magic of Conflict.* Simon and Schuster.

Csikszentmihalyi, M. (1990). *Flow: The Psychology of Optimal Experience.* Harper & Row.

Csikszentmihalyi, M. (1997). *Finding Flow: The Psychology of Engagement with Everyday Life.* Basic Books.

Dreher, D. (1997). *The Tao of Personal Leadership.* Harper Business.

Fletcher, J. (March, 2001). "Invisible Work: The Disappearing of Relational Practice at Work." Simmons College Center for Gender in Organizations.

Goleman, D. (1995). *Emotional Intelligence: Why It Can Matter More Than IQ.* Bantam.

Goleman, D. (1998). *Working With Emotional Intelligence.* Bantam.

Goleman, D. (Nov/Dec,1998) "What Makes a Leader?" *Harvard Business* Review, pg. 93-102. Harvard Business School Press.

Heider, J., et al. (1984). *The Tao of Leadership: Lao Tzu's Tao Te Ching Adapted for a New Age.* Humanics Partners.

Katie, B., & Mitchell, S. (2002). *Loving What Is.* Three Rivers Press.

Peters, T. (1988). *Thriving on Chaos.* Perennial Press.

Tzu, S. (translated by Griffith, Samuel B.). (1963). *The Art of War.* Oxford University Press.

Welch, J. (2001). *Straight from the Gut.* Warner Business Books.

Wheatley, M. (1992). *Leadership and the New Science.* Berrett-Koehler.

Chapter 3
FLOWING LEADERSHIP

The flowing rhythm has a "fluid, circular, continuous motion" that embodies constantly shifting sound and movement like a meandering river or an undulating snake, sinuous, able to change direction when needed but generally progressing slowly, yet inexorably, toward a goal. The hallmark of the flowing rhythm is contiguity—each movement being connected to the next in a clear and obvious way. The hip moves and passes the movement on to the waist; from the waist, the movement flows up the spine; from the spine, the movement flows out the shoulders to the elbows, arms, hands and fingers; the fingers connect to the hip transferring the energy flow back to the hip causing more contiguous movement in similar or other directions. All movement is grounded, earthy, and clear.

Metaphorically, flowing is about knowing your core self and moving from that place—grounded in your values. It's knowing yourself in connection to others, to the earth, and to all-that-is. Roth writes, "Michael Jordan playing basketball is the essence of flowing. His internal rhythm connects with the energies of the ball, his team, his opponents, and the court, until they all merge into one organic entity and it becomes as natural for the ball to swoosh through the net as it is for breath to flow in and out of our bodies."

The Flowing leader takes things one step at a time—seeing how each movement informs and causes the next. These leaders take their time to assess where the movement is in their organization. They think through their decisions and behaviors and move their organizations slowly, yet inevitably towards certain objectives. These leaders are careful to avoid blocking the flow, knowing the power required to stop movement is much greater than the power needed to channel it into desired directions. Their goal is to guide the energy of their organizations to move in ways consistent with the organizing purpose. Movement is visible, extraverted—yet one has the sense that the energy has a force below it that keeps it moving through designated channels no matter what.

In his study of creative geniuses, psychologist Mihaly Csikszentmihalyi wrote about 'flow' as a state of deep focus that occurs when people engage in challenging tasks that demand intense concentration and commitment. Flow occurs when a person's skill level is perfectly balanced to the challenge level of a task that has clear goals and provides immediate feedback. A flow state ensues when one is engaged in self-controlled, goal-related, meaningful actions.

Flowing is an externalized movement to the rhythm of the inner drummer, focused on their own activities, goals, or purpose. Others are often attracted to that sense of enacted purpose and follow them, want to support them, be like them—thus they are leading because their behavior demonstrates the power of tapping into and moving from a sense of shared values and purpose.

MOTHER TERESA

Mother Teresa exemplifies the Flowing leadership style. Mother Teresa had a slow but steady approach to providing service leadership in her chosen arena. She determined from an early age that her vocation was to serve the poorest of the poor, and she never wavered from that conviction. Her good deeds were indisputable even though some criticized her for her conservative views on abortion and her willingness to turn a blind eye to questionable donations. She was as undeterred by criticism as she was by any other challenges to her mission, responding, "No matter who says what, you should accept it with a smile and do your own work." Her approach was simple and humble, and she spoke softly—but she was also known to ask hard questions about whether-how we were living our lives consistent with our values. The alignment between her actions and message resonated with people all around the world. Over the years she drew larger crowds, won the Nobel Peace Prize, and grew her service ministries with this style.

We often lead in situations that call for our skills and commitment to make a significant difference. Situations that call forth our leadership are likely to be times of crisis, conflict, change, confusion, and/or chaos. The Flowing leadership style can be effective in times of evolutionary change—change that is inexorable, continuous and relatively clear.

You know what must be done—it's often fairly simple to determine what must be done in such situations. But it may not be easy to do what must be done for many different reasons. It may require too much effort for too long such that is it too hard to sustain that effort. It may seem that you are not making much difference because the results are not externally evident. Perhaps the more you do, the more you are asked to do. You may have feelings, expectations, commitments to others, or relationships that make it hard to do what you need to do. Or it may require that you change some habit. It may also mean that you have to march to your own drummer while everyone around you is telling you that you should do things their way.

KAREN ROBERTS

Let's take the example of Karen Roberts. From the time she was a little girl, Karen knew she wanted to be a doctor because she wanted to help people live healthier lives. She really cared that poor people of any-all kinds received respectful care. She is a bright African-American woman with a big heart who attended

Ivy-league medical schools and earned top-notch medical credentials. Every summer, however, she provided medical care to poor and people of color in various places. When she received her MD, she could practice medicine almost anywhere given her skills and credentials, and make a lot of money at the same time. Her family, friends, and colleagues often thought she should go for it—since she could. But she'd always known where her commitment as a healer lay. She decided to practice, in her respectful caring connected style, in a large urban hospital-clinic that serves a demographically diverse community—taking a position and salary that were not as high as some of the other offers she received.

It was hard to stay the course over the last 20 years—in part because poor people and people of color often did not have the resources they needed to sustain any assistance she gave them so results were not evident, and partly because she didn't always have the resources she needed to make a positive difference. Many challenges had to do with patients' at-home habits—the only way she could influence them was to build a relationship of trust so that the patient would take the non-medical advice as seriously as they did the medical treatments. Other challenges had to do with systematic and community diseases which she addressed by participating fully in her community. And through it all, she was sometimes tempted to serve in more economically privileged areas—even going so far at to take such a job for a couple of years in order to see if she could walk the logical and easy path—rather than her true, simple, but hard path. She returned.

Recently, she was honored by a Jewish community group for her service. One of the most touching stories told about her was of a man who was concerned that he would not be able to be with his family member during the Sabbath while that family member was being treated in the hospital. He mentioned this to Karen as the attending physician, and she just said, "I'll take care of it",—and he was allowed to stay. The man was pleased to know that she cared enough to listen, and more importantly that she followed through. Karen did not even remember the situation. Many other people shared how she had been present, competent, respectful, caring, and just 'there'—and she saw herself 'just doing her work'. She also became a role model for other health-care providers in the facility. An urban hospital known for its caring-competent staff—its service to serving the poor and communities of color. Karen made a significant difference, doing her work, one step at time, over 20 years—using a Flowing leadership style.

Karen Roberts is an example of everyday leader—someone deciding to make a difference and then just doing it. Throughout this book, I will provide examples of everyday leaders, like Karen Roberts, as well as famous leaders who typify each leadership style, as I did with Mother Teresa. In the case of the Flowing style, two other famous leaders come to mind—Cleopatra and Mary Magdalene.

CLEOPATRA

Most people have heard the story of Cleopatra, Queen of Egypt. In the popular mind, she is thought of as a beautiful woman who gained and sacrificed much through her love of two powerful men. Cleopatra, the last of the Ptolemaic Dynasty, reigned in Egypt from 51 to 30 BCE. Her family was not Egyptian, but rather descendents of a Macedonian commander, Ptolemy, who served under Alexander the Great. At 18 years old, Cleopatra co-inherited an indebted Egypt upon her father's death. A very intelligent and observant girl growing up, she had ample opportunity to observe the machinations of power within the royal entourage, and to learn at close hand that Roman power was to be feared. So, although Cleopatra was born into the royal family, she knew she had to set and stay focused on her goals if she were to survive. She had several goals in her reign:

- to keep Egypt from being swallowed up by Rome;
- to repay the debts to Rome;

- to become a wealthy kingdom;
- to regain some of the lands her father lost during his reign;
- to put an end to civil war and strife in the kingdom; and
- to rule Egypt—alone.

She achieved all of these goals. To do so, she won the loyalty of her subjects and engaged in 'strategic alliances' with her would-be conquerors, the Romans. She is known to have had relationships Julius Caesar and Mark Anthony—both powerful, ambitious Roman leaders. Her alliances with these men greatly served her goals. When Julius Caesar came to collect on the Roman debt and end the civil war caused by the dispute between her and her brothers, she convinced him to combine armies, resources, and strategies with her. Her alliance as equals kept Roman power working with her, rather than subjugating her. They conquered other kingdoms (which greatly enlarged Cleopatra's kingdom and gave her money to repay the debts) and defeated her brother (which ended the civil war and put her on the throne alone). To win the loyalty of her subjects, she was the first of her dynasty to learn and speak the language of her would-be conquerors and her subjects. She spoke at least 9 languages. She used the powerful religious symbolism of the time, minting a coin of her suckling Caesaria—the son she bore Julius Caesar—evoking the image of her as a reincarnation of the goddess, Isis, with her son Horus. She dressed as a male Pharoah in ceremonies, symbolically affirming her divine right to rule alone as any man would.

MARY MAGDALENE

Mary Magdalene makes an interesting contrast to Cleopatra as a Flowing style leader. Like Cleopatra, our image of her has been greatly influenced by the writings of people who reluctantly admit to her charismatic influence. Cleopatra's story comes to us mostly through the writings of a man who was a propagandist for Cleopatra's enemy. Despite the fact that he was charged with making her look like a power-hungry harlot, his admiration for her abilities still shines through his reports of her activities. Similarly, Mary Magdalene was obviously too important a person in Jesus of Nazareth's circle to leave out, yet her name has become (erroneously many current biblical scholars say) synonymous with harlotry.

Biblical scholars assert that there is nothing actually written in the Bible to support the idea that Mary Magdalene was actually a prostitute at any point in her life. She is, however, called "the companion" of Jesus in the Gospel of Philip. Many scholars note, that it is agreed by those reporting on the life of Jesus, that Mary Magdalene and his mother Mary were among Jesus' constant companions. Moreover, Mary Magdalene is referred to as the 'Apostle of Apostles' because she was the first one to carry the 'good news' (e.g. gospel) that Jesus was resurrected. After Jesus' ascent, Mary Magdalene traveled far and wide continuing to teach Jesus' message to people. She traveled as far as southern France, they say, where she converted the royal family, as well as the local populace. So where did Mary Magdalene come from? Why did she hang out so much with Jesus? And how did her strong commitment to him and his teachings become sexualized (and diminished)?

In Jesus' time, people were often named for their town, their profession, and/or the lineage-parentage. The name Mary was one of the most common names for girls used in the region, and there are many "Marys" in the Bible. Some say "Magdalene" means simply "one from the town of Magdala." During the time when Magdalene would have lived, there was no town called Magdala; this was a name given by Crusaders in an effort to match places in the Holy Land with Biblical accounts. Others tend to interpret the root of the word, "magdala," or "magdal" or "migdal" to "tower" or "fortress," and base the meaning of her name on the word rather than the town. Margaret Starbird wrote in her books that she believes that "Magdalene" was an epitaph, which would mean "Mary, the Tower," metaphorically making Mary Magdalene a tower of strength for early Christians, if not for Jesus himself.

Recent thinking about Mary Magdalene is that she was a woman of means converted early to the teachings of Jesus. She, as was not uncommon during that time, contributed her resources to Jesus' efforts and left her home to follow him as a disciple, just like the other disciples were called to do. Because the Bible is translated, is missing texts that were part of the original, and is composed of a series of writings often done long after the people and events written about were dead, we cannot always get a clear picture of what actually happened. For instance, the word that is translated as 'companion' referring to Mary's relationship to Jesus, has also been translated as 'consort'. There is also reference to Jesus kissing Mary Magdalene on the mouth, a behavior he is not reported to have done with any of his male disciples. Yet some scholars translate that kiss to mean an apostolic transmission, rather than a sign of affection to his 'consort'. Additionally, Mary Magdalene was written about as the "Bride of Christ", though biblical scholars argue that might be a figurative rather than literal teaching. What seems to be consistent and clear is that Mary Magdalene and Jesus were close, and that she traveled and learned from him as did the other male disciples.

So, how did she become the redeemed prostitute in our collective mythology? And why? The leading theory is that Pope Gregory the Great intentionally changed her identity, perhaps reflecting what was already popular opinion. As I mentioned earlier, Mary was a very common name and there are many references to various Marys in the Bible. It has been suggested that Mary Magdalene was mixed up with Mary of Bethany and the anonymous sinner (who was presumed to be a prostitute) of Luke who anointed Jesus' feet. So it might have just been too hard to keep all the Marys straight. But then, why would Church leaders let people persist in the error for someone so important?

In early Christian texts that contain both Mary Magdalene and Peter, she and Peter seem to be at odds with each other. During Jesus' time they were probably able to work that out but the impression of a rivalry between Peter and Mary Magdalene was reported often enough that scholars take the rivalry seriously. After Jesus' death, Mary went on to spread the gospels (as did all of the disciples). Her approach and teachings emphasized an egalitarian, liberating Christianity where women were valued as much as men, and could as easily be leaders in the church as well as men. Her teachings and approach are often described in Gnostic texts. Peter and Paul's teachings, which are the teachings that have had the most influence on the Western Christian Church, were more authoritarian and patriarchal—where women had more subordinate roles to men.

Cleopatra and Mary Magdalene, as Flowing style leaders, both had clear goals which they pursued, one step at a time, despite what people of their time might have thought they could or should do. They both had a strong commitment to enacting what they believed in. Both, as strong women, made a significant difference in their time on their terms—in situations where some of their challenge was to stay themselves as fully feminine, and make their contribution as leaders from their core.

REFERENCES

CASE: Mother Theresa
 Chalika, J., & LeJoly, E., (Eds.). (1996). *The Joy in Loving: A Guide to Daily Living with Mother Theresa.* Putnum.

CLIENT: Karen Roberts
All client examples are provided by real people whose names have been changed for confidentiality reasons.

CASE: Cleopatra
>> Plutarch, S., P. & Waterfield, R. (1999*). Roman Lives: A Selection of Eight Lives.* Oxford University Press.

>> "Constructing Charisma: Cleopatra, Queen of Egypt."
>> (1994). Leadership case by the Hartwick Humanities in Management Institute at Hartwick College. Oneonta, N.Y.

>> PBS Video Program. (Aired 2001). *Cleopatra: First Woman of Power.*

CASE: Mary Magdalene
>> *The Gospel of Philip.*
>> CITATION 1: "And the companion of the [...] Mary Magdalene. [...] loved her more than all the disciples, and used to kiss her often on her mouth. The rest of the disciples [...]. They said to him 'Why do you love her more than all of us?'"
>> CITATION 2: "There were three who always walked with the Lord: Mary, his mother, and her sister, and Magdalene, the one who was called his companion. His sister and his mother and his companion were each a Mary."

>> Graham Brock, A. (2002). *Mary Magdalene, The First Apostle: The Struggle for Authority.* Harvard University Press.

Chapter 4
STACCATO LEADERSHIP

Staccato builds from, yet contrasts sharply with, Flowing. Where Flowing is Yin, Staccato is Yang. Flowing is Tai Chi; Staccato is Kung Fu. Where Flowing is archetypically feminine, earthy energy; Staccato is archetypically masculine, fire energy. Flowing takes in from the center; Staccato puts out. Roth describes staccato as "short, sharp, percussive—stops and starts," bursts of energy moving in various directions. A classic example of staccato movement from dance would be flamenco—the stamping, dramatic dance of Spanish gypsies. Staccato is dancing with your bones, creating all kinds of angles and edges like geometry in motion. Lines erupt out of curves, articulating our separateness, creating walls or breaking them down.

Metaphorically, Staccato is about getting in touch with your energy, your passion, and expressing that passionate energy to others, projecting your self into the outside world. Staccato is about doing, not just being; taking action, not just thinking about it. It is directing the flow of energy into clear-cut lines. Any disciplined activity in which you move according to specific rules such as skiing, swimming, diving, rock climbing, yoga or ballet, 12-step programs, learning piano—all can use that staccato energy. It is the spirit of rock-n-roll; a masculine-without-mercy energy, the untamed yearn for freedom.

As a leadership style, Staccato is a very extraverted "push" style—where leaders assert, direct, coerce, and tell folks what needs to be done. Staccato style leaders break rules, take risks, experiment, challenge the status quo, go for the gold, take action—in short they do! Some Staccato style leaders love dramatic flair with their actions; they come in, shake things up, and get everyone energized and moving. Direction of movement is not always as important as taking some action, doing something! The Staccato style may also be clear about drawing in the lines, the boundaries, setting the goals, protecting their key people—while still pushing folks to do what needs to be done. For many of us, Staccato is 'the' leadership style leaders should have—its masculine command-control aspects are familiar in our general assumptions of how leaders lead. Staccato leaders know they are making a difference—they intend to and they do. And many entrepreneurs seem to resonate to this style; for example Madame CJ Walker.

MADAME C. J. WALKER

> *I got myself a start by giving myself a start*, said Madame CJ Walker. *I am a woman who came from the cotton fields of the South. I was promoted from there to the washtub. Then I was promoted to the cook kitchen, and from there I promoted myself into the business of manufacturing hair goods and preparations.... I have built my own factory on my own ground.*

Madame C. J. Walker is the first black self-made millionaire woman in the U.S. She is credited with marketing the "hot comb," (a steel comb that when heated, straightens curly and kinky hair making it easier to manage and style), selling and promoting her hair care products, and establishing beauty schools to train women about her "Walker System" and business in general. She not only promoted herself to a position of empowered

44

business executive, she helped many other women promote themselves similarly.

Sarah Breedlove *(1867-1919)* was born and raised poor to ex-slave sharecroppers in Delta, Louisiana. Due to stress, poor living conditions, inadequate diet and damaging hair preparation techniques, Sarah started losing her hair. Existing hair products did not help her condition. In response to a "vision from God", she mixed some ingredients and created a hair growing formula that stopped her hair loss and even spurred hair growth. She shared her hair care formula with other black women, along with some special tools she developed to facilitate hair styling, and began marketing the treatments as "The Walker System".

Sarah Breedlove eventually married Charles Joseph (CJ) Walker, a newspaperman who had knowledge of advertising and mail order procedures. CJ Walker, her second husband, helped her design her advertisements and set up a mail-order operation for the fledgling business. Walker's husband had a smaller vision than she did for the business potential. This eventually led to their separation. She continued to use the initials of his name after the dissolution of the marriage. At the time, whites frequently called black women by their first names no matter who they were, so black women would keep their first names a secret, if possible. Hence, she is referred to as Madame C. J. Walker rather than Sarah Breedlove Walker.

As the business grew, Walker hired former maids, farm laborers, housewives, and school teachers to fill jobs at all levels from factory worker to commissioned sales agents. Walker not only provided jobs for blacks, but others obtained jobs as a result of the improvement in their appearance.

You have opened up a trade for hundreds of colored women to make an honest and profitable living where they make as much in one week as a month's salary would bring from any other position that a colored woman can secure, wrote an agent in 1913.

Walker made sure her sales agents were trained to use, demonstrate, and sell the products. She taught these women how to set up beauty shops in their homes and how to keep the account books. To foster cooperation among the agents, Walker created a national organization called the Hair Culturists Union of America and organized the first federation of black hair-care and cosmetics manufacturers.

Staccato leaders like Madame CJ Walker are willing to challenge existing notions of what's possible, and push for change in that status quo. The Staccato leadership style also seems to be very effective in situations that call for quick, clear, surgical responses—periods of crisis or emergency situations. People call on Staccato leaders when something must be done—it may not be pleasant, but it must occur in order for the organization to be healthier afterwards. In such cases, the leader is often expected to make difficult, even unpopular decisions, which results (hopefully) in long-term improvement despite the short-term pain or loss. It is also common for people who resonate to this style to expect sacrifices, and to make sacrifices in the pursuit of a shared goal. In the *Art of War* below, Sun Tzu's general clearly takes advantage of his soldiers' willingness to sacrifice themselves for the cause. In the example following the *Art of War,* Jack Welch expects sacrifices from his workers and makes personal relationship sacrifices himself while scoring enormous economical victories.

SUN TZU – THE ART OF WAR

The *Art of War*, a text written by Sun Tzu over 2500 years ago in China, provides valuable tactical advice to leaders using the Staccato leadership style. The *Art of War* is prescribed reading for many military leader and is a popular text in business schools. Sun Tzu talks about the importance of surprise, of doing what must be done even when folks don't like it, even cutting off retreats when that is necessary. Sun Tzu describes the details of appropriate leader action in specific situations. Some of his suggestions include:

Doing Battle (Waging War). When doing battle, seek a quick victory. A protracted battle will blunt weapons and dampen ardor. If troops lay siege to a walled city, their strength will be exhausted. If the army is exposed to a prolonged campaign, the nation's resources will not suffice. When weapons are blunted, and ardor dampened, strength exhausted, and resources depleted, the neighboring rulers will take advantage of these complications. Then even the wisest of counsels would not be able to avert the consequences that must ensue. ...No nation has ever benefited from protracted warfare.

...Generally in warfare, keeping a nation intact is best, (to ruin it is inferior to this); Therefore, to gain a hundred victories in a hundred battles is not the highest excellence (the acme of skill); to subjugate the enemy's army without doing battle is the highest of excellence (the acme of skill). Therefore, the best strategy is to attack the enemy's plans, next is to attack alliances, next is to attack the army, and the worst is to attack a walled city. Therefore, one who is skilled in warfare principles subdues the enemy without doing battle, takes the enemy's walled city without attacking, and overthrows the enemy quickly, without protracted warfare. (Your aim must be to take All-under-Heaven intact. Thus your troops are not worn out and your gains will be complete. This is the art of offensive strategy.)

...One who knows when he can fight, and when he cannot fight, will be victorious...; one who knows how to unite upper and lower ranks in purpose will be victorious; ... One who knows the enemy and knows himself will not be in danger in a hundred battles. One who does not know the enemy but knows himself will sometimes win, sometimes lose. One who does not know the enemy and does not know himself will be in danger in every battle. ...know the

enemy's plans and calculate their strengths and weaknesses. Provoke him, to know his patterns of movement. Determine his position, to know the ground of death and of life. Probe him, to know where he is strong and where he is weak...

...Do not attack an enemy that has the high ground; do not attack an enemy that has his back to a hill; do not pursue feigned retreats; do not attack elite troops; do not swallow the enemy's bait; do not thwart an enemy retreating home. If you surround the enemy, leave an outlet; do not press an enemy that is cornered. These are the principles of warfare.

...Throw your troops into situations where there is no escape, where they will die before escaping. When they are about to die, what can they not do? They will exert their full strength. When the troops are in desperate situations, they fear nothing; having penetrated deep in enemy ground, they are united. When there are no other alternatives, they will fight. Therefore, though not disciplined, they are alert; though not asked, they are devoted; though without promises, they are faithful; and though not commanded, they are trustworthy. Prohibit omens, and get rid of doubts, and they will die without any other thoughts.

...the nature of the army is to defend when surrounded, to fight hard when there are no other alternatives, and to obey commands promptly when in danger.

...command the masses like commanding one person. Give your troops tasks, but do not reveal your plans to them. Get them to face danger, but do not reveal the advantages. Throw them into danger and they will survive; put them on deadly ground and they will live. Only if the troops are in situations of danger will they turn defeat into victory.

Sometimes Staccato leadership can feel like this—where decisions are made based on the tactics that will help reach a bigger long term goal, but the individuals may feel somewhat like invisible pawns on a giant chessboard. Yet, many people are willing to sign up to follow leaders with this style in the service of a cherished goal. Those who survive and win are often thrilled about their victory—those who do not survive may be honored for their sacrifice. In such situations, with winners and losers, you will also have the range of human responses to winning and losing. Many will see the result and appreciate the leadership styles—others may think the costs were too high.

JACK WELCH

Jack Welch, a well known business leader with the Staccato style is such a controversial leader. Neutron Jack, as he has been called, is the former CEO of one of the most complex organizations in the world—General Electric. He is credited with having transformed what was an old-line American industrial giant into a keenly competitive global organization. Welch reshaped the company through more than 600 acquisitions—firmly selling off businesses that were not the best in their industries and buying-keeping-investing in those companies/divisions that were the best in their market. He was able to exercise considerable influence and power over a far flung and complex organization—a company with over (US) $300 billion in assets, almost $100 billion in revenue, and over 275 million employees in more than 100 countries. He squeezed 350 product lines into 12 big businesses, shed 9 billion dollars worth of assets and spent 18 billion dollars on acquisitions—eliminating 100,000 jobs while making the stock holders happy with improvements in all key financial indicators.

Welch sought and wielded power and authority widely throughout GE. He was the head honcho and everybody knew it. He was a strong taskmaster and set high performance standards. One such standard was the requirement that a company-division be #1 or #2 in their market in order for that company-division to be able to stay in the GE company family (not be sold off). One of his books is entitled *Get Better or Get Beaten—31 leadership secrets from Jack Welch.* He also supported and promoted others like him, those who had "E to the 4th power": enormous personal ENERGY, the ability to ENERGIZE others, an instinctively competitive EDGE, and the skill to EXECUTE their decisions.

Welch's ability to set goals, to focus everyone's attention on those goals, to reward those who followed his direction with gusto and to punish those who didn't, to sacrifice some things (people?) in order to win, and to do all of this with incredible energy – these are all strong indicators of the Staccato leadership style.

ELIZABETH VARGAS

In our third example, Elizabeth Vargas, we have a modern super-woman challenging the notion that an ambitious woman must sacrifice either family or work while acknowledging that attaining work-life balance with this intense-passionate style can be a never-ending challenge. While she shares the passionate energy typical of the Staccato style we read about in the previous two male examples, she also brings forth a point that is important to keep in mind. The Staccato style is essentially masculine—and men in US-Western culture have more latitude in expressing this style and remaining effective than women typically do. Where a man with a command-control-take-charge style might be called an assertive powerful leader, a woman who uses this style without softening it somewhat might be called something completely different. Both men and women tend to expect women to soften assertive, 'push' behavior.

For instance, Elizabeth Vargas, ABC news anchor, has a job that requires her to ask tough questions and do probing analysis. An article written about her in <u>Hispanic</u> magazine after she won an award in June, 2004, Liz Llorente says Vargas "exudes a smart, thoughtful and authoritative air …steadiness… [and is] penetrating and persistent, *but always polite…* with a characteristic style of *calmly rolling out a grenade* of a question [in interviews]."

She loves provocative, complex topics (like religion, politics and diversity) and she is willing to ruffle feathers and shake people out of their comfort zones.

She's a wife, mother and super-journalist, working 6-days a week, and long hours. One of her friends describes her as one of the most driven, anal people she knows. "She gets up before 5 a.m. with her baby, runs into ABC to work, studies like a maniac for future stories, comes back home to be with her husband and baby, and fits in working out. Elizabeth acknowledges her passionate commitment to her work, mentioning how proud she was of risky stories she's done. One such story challenged previous assumptions about Mary Magdalene. Another contrasted the media silence about a Latina and an African American woman who disappeared around the same time as a white woman, Laci Peterson. Vargas challenged experts and journalists to examine why the women of color's stories were barely covered by mainstream media while the white woman's story was in the news media constantly. Elizabeth Vargas is clear that she wants to see equitable representation for everyone in the media and to spur people to take action to change things when they are not fair. She's willing to break norms, take risks, challenge prevailing wisdom, and push—politely—to make that happen.

The Staccato leaders have passionate energy they direct towards the achievement of key goals. They are willing and able to focus their and others' energy, even sacrificing things/people important to them in the service of achieving these goals. It's a command-control, win-lose, clear and competitive style. Sun Tzu's general wins the war by any means necessary. Entrepreneurs like Madame CJ Walker manifest their dreams with gusto, overcoming any and all obstacles. And Welch and Vargas demonstrate that incredible extraverted energy also typical of Staccato leaders.

The next three leadership styles – Chaos, Lyrical and Stillness – are new ways to think of leading and leadership for many of us. Flowing and Staccato leadership are familiar, goal directed styles where leaders seem to have and maintain some mastery of their followers and themselves, as well as a clear understanding of the situation and what must be done to achieve shared goals. In the remaining three leadership styles, one is called to make a difference without control (especially in Chaos), authority (especially in Lyrical), or a straightforward understanding of the situation (especially with the light-dark complexity in Stillness).

REFERENCES

CASE: Madame C.J. Walker
> Kathleen, D. (March, 1989). "Madame C.J. Walker: First Black Woman Millionaire." *American History Illustrated.* *Vol. 24*, 24-25.

> Bundles, A. (2002). *On Her Own Ground: The Life and Times of Madame C.J. Walker*. Scribner.

> Lowry, B. (2003). *Her Dream of Dreams: The Rise and Triumph of Madame C.J. Walker*. Knopf.

CASE: Sun Tzu
> Tzu, S. (S. Griffith, Trans.). (1963; 1991). *The Art of War*. Oxford University Press. (The excerpts from the *Art of War* in the text are a blend of the Sonshi.com and Griffith translations.)

"Sun Tzu's The Art of War." (1994). Leadership case
published by Hartwick Humanities in Management
Institute at Hartwick College. Oneonta, N.Y.

CASE: Jack Welch

Welch, J. (2001). *Straight from the Gut*. Warner Business
Books.

Slater, R. (2003). *29 Leadership Secrets from Jack Welch*.
McGraw-Hill.

Krames, J. (2001). *The Jack Welch Lexicon of Leadership:
Over 250 Terms, Concepts, Strategies and
Initiatives of the Legendary Leader*. McGraw-Hill.

CASE: Elizabeth Vargas

Cover Story: *Latinas of Excellence*. (June 2004). Retrieved
from http://www.hispanicmagazine.com.

Chapter 5
CHAOS LEADERSHIP

The chaos rhythm shares the high, energy of staccato but without the control of form or direction. To resonate with this rhythm a person must be comfortable with ambiguity, letting the music cause the movement to control the direction the body takes, knowing that in some situations the body is smarter than the brain. The body and music blend in ways that maximize efficiency. In music, externalized chaos is the polyphonic rhythms of African drums. Chaos is internalized in the arrhythmic Arabic taksim—music that seems to be without a clear beat or form to follow yet still propels you to express it.

The word chaos actually means "empty space" or abyss in Greek. Roth describes this empty space is a place of creative potential. Chaos is the place where contraries meet, mix, and dissolve...where opposites meet and clash, unleashing force-energy. It is a space of creative shaping-shaped creativity, of passionate commitment-committed passion, of innocent wisdom-wise innocence. It is the gateway to the intuitive mind-body-heart; that part of us that knows our destiny, our purpose, our contribution, our presents (presence), our Self.

Chaos implies out of control. Chaos tends to get a bad rap in our culture since we seem to want to understand and control most aspects of our lives. Often the result when we meet that creative force in empty space we are afraid of the abyss. To reduce our fear we try to shape the emptiness.

The Chaos leader is challenged because they understand the expectation from followers that they must *seem* to be in control; yet they feel strongly that having control, at least that externalized sense of being in charge of the situation most people consider control, is impossible. A large part of their energy goes to helping themselves and others feel more comfortable with the idea that chaotic situations often require relinquishing, at least for some period of time, that sense of being in control.

Chaos leaders know that followers need to explore entirely new ways of being and doing that come from within them—to surrender, letting action emerge from the demands of the situation, rather than planning and controlling every organizational move. These leaders know they do not have control, do not have all the answers, cannot save everyone, maybe not even themselves—but on some deeper level they believe in people, they believe in their purpose (even a divine purpose), and they have a deep trust in the Universe-God-Spirit-Divine Organizing principles. Chaos leaders often take a degree of pleasure in smashing the boxes and boundaries many of us hide in so that we feel safe and in control. They show us how the categories we live with may be comfortable at times, but way too tight if we really want to grow and/or solve our more complex problems. Staccato leaders may also smash the boxes—but they usually recreate boxes-forms-structures; ones they feel are better than what existed before. The Staccato leader appreciates the value of structure for guiding people's efforts in desired directions. The Chaos leader is more likely to expect us to think-live outside the box altogether. That box might be our working habits in our organizations, our social identities—such as race, gender, social class, nationality, age, ethnicity, religion—our assumptions about how best to organize and relate to each other, or our basic assumptions about what matters in daily lives. The

Chaos leader examples I will provide in this chapter have all challenged some fundamental conceptions of who we-they are.

As a result of their challenges, people involved with the leader at all levels—front-line personnel, supervisors, and managers—and in many areas of life—art, religion, politics, business, etc.—are empowered to respond immediately and effectively to the needs of the situation. We get to know ourselves and our limits better—both who we are, and who we are not. The Chaos leader stands with courage and exemplifies the idea that we can stand at the edge of the abyss, even let go and be in the chaos itself, and still we exist. Chaos leaders are able to stay/stand/be present in the midst of the storm or the emptiness—and not disappear psychologically, emotionally, or physically. His or her ability to stand it, literally, encourages (gives heart to) others.

BAYARD RUSTIN

Take for instance, Bayard Rustin (1912-1987). Rustin, was a civil rights organizer, political activist, master strategist, African American, and 'known homosexual'. Rustin was born in West Chester, Pennsylvania on March 17. He was raised by his grandmother in a Quaker community. In school, he excelled in both academics and sports. It was on a trip to an out of town football game that Rustin first experienced racism when he was refused service in a restaurant. Rustin got involved in the U.S. civil rights movement and was a major player in it throughout the 1950's.

In February 1956, when Bayard Rustin arrived in Montgomery to assist with the nascent bus boycott, Martin Luther King, Jr. had not personally embraced nonviolence. In fact, there were guns inside King's house, and armed guards posted at his doors. Rustin persuaded boycott leaders to adopt complete nonviolence, teaching them Gandhian nonviolent direct protest. He worked closely with Martin Luther King, Jr. and A. Phillip Randolph in laying the foundations for the non-violence of the

57

civil rights movement for which King is so widely known. Rustin was an instrumental advisor to King in organizing the Southern Christian Leadership Conference (SCLC) in 1956. Rustin was also fun-loving, mischievous, artistic, gifted with a fine singing voice, and known as an art collector who sometimes found museum-quality pieces in New York City trash. One of his favorite quotes was "I believe in social dislocation and creative trouble."

BILL CLINTON

Another leader who comes to mind for the Chaos style is William Jefferson (Bill) Clinton. Very few leaders could stand to, or stand and, lead amid a period as chaotic as the eight years he spent as U.S. President. He led during a period of rapid economic growth, expanding government, attacks on his personal character, and family turmoil. Amid it all he kept his affability, purpose, and personal clarity—but mostly he stood there, poised, smiling, and present amid all the swirling energy around him. He committed adultery and was charged with sexual harassment; he eventually admitted to adultery and still kept the support of family members, women voters and women staffers. He lied, then apologized for lying-sinning, and was 'forgiven' by many because of his repentance. He was ridiculed regularly by media comedians and joined in by quipping and making jokes about his own behavior. He loved the role of president, saying "I may not have been the greatest president, but I've had the most fun eight years" even though he was constantly challenged as a leader by Whitewater, by the Lewinsky scandal, and an impeachment. He was beloved and hated but through it all, he stayed—himself—a man from a single-parent household, a born poor-working class-saxophone playing-McDonalds-and-junk-food-loving boy from Arkansas, as well as a Rhodes Scholar, and popular Democratic re-elected U.S. President.

Clinton was able to make connections to people and events in unexpected ways. Some say he brilliantly navigated the "white waters"—that chaotic energy of his presidency—by allowing his instincts about the body politic. He especially relied on the good will and humanity of the every-day voters who elected him to guide him to the right action at the right time. He allowed order emerged from the chaos—an effective response when even pretense to control is not possible. Despite the chaos energy surrounding his presidency, his overall record of achievements, especially the economy, is very strong. For many people, his ability to withstand the whitewater, to achieve so many shared goals, to keep his charismatic charm while affirming his humble roots is encouraging. These are hallmarks of effective Chaos leadership.

ALBERT EINSTEIN

In the realm of science, Albert Einstein is an example of a Chaos style leader. Paradoxically, Einstein, the iconic iconoclast, the science clown, the antiauthoritarian authority—who quipped "To punish me for my contempt for authority, Fate made me an authority myself." -- did not like chaos. *Time Magazine*, in their report of Einstein as the person of the 20th century, described him as someone who combined rare genius with a deep moral sense and a total indifference to convention. He started life being seen as a slow learner because he talked late and at least one teacher thought he was unlikely to become much of anything. But through a series of thought experiments where he considered the nature of the universe, he developed theories and raised questions-possibilities that have kept physicists busy for over half a century. Four of his most widely known contributions are:

➤ Wave-particle duality of light. Light behaves like both a wave and a stream of particles. The stream of particles is called quanta or photons. Einstein won the Nobel Prize for this theory that became the foundation of quantum physics.

➤ The special theory of relativity. No matter how fast you are moving toward or away from a source of light, the speed of that light beam will appear the same, a constant 186,000 miles per second. But space and time will appear relative—that is, as you approach the speed of light, time will slow down from your perspective and you will get shorter and heavier. In short, space and time are not fixed, but relative and pliable.

➢ Energy and matter. Energy and matter are different forms of the same thing as expressed in the famous $e=mc^2$ equation. This equation explained why an atomic bomb was possible and helped us understand many other things such as why the sky is blue (because of how air molecules diffuse sunlight).

➢ The general theory of relativity. Gravity is a warping of space-time that happens in the presence of mass. First, we have to give up the idea that gravity is a force as Newton put forth and we believed since the 18th century. Then we also have space-time, not just space and/or time. And third, time and space are not fixed, they are relative. Physicist Steven Hawking describes this theory as requiring us to give up the idea that there is a universal quantity that all clocks measure, called time; and, instead, accept the idea that everyone has their own personal time. Our clocks would agree if we are at rest with respect to each other but not if we are moving. The general theory of relativity also asserts that light always takes the shortest possible route from one point to another. So when starlight passes near the sun, the shortest route is a curved line that follows the curvature of space-time making the starlight appear as if it is coming from a different point than its actual origin. If the mass is very concentrated, the curvature of space-time becomes infinite and a light beam that comes too close will never escape—that is called a black hole. When physicists were able to demonstrate that the general theory of relativity works, they were aware that Einstein had made a revolutionary contribution to our understanding.

The confirmation of the general theory of relativity made Einstein world famous. But Einstein responded to all the hoopla surrounding the confirmation of his theory with humorous detachment. Einstein was a complex man with many contradictions. It is reported that his private life was different from his public persona. He was warmhearted and cold, a doting father and an aloof mate, a flirt deeply concerned with strangers yet he would withdraw from intimacy, and he kept a lifelong suspicion of all authority.

In his thought experiments, Einstein asked questions others never seriously considered. His contributions to quantum physics opened the door to aspects of quantum theory where even he left his comfort zone. Subsequent quantum physicists eventually concluded that wave particle duality means there is a randomness or uncertainty in nature. This idea made Einstein very uncomfortable. He is quoted as having quipped "God does not play dice." Because he believed in both universal order on the big scale and relativity at the subatomic level (with its apparent randomness), he searched for a way to join those two levels of understanding in a unified theory. Einstein died before he could find a unified theory but his belief in one keeps physicists in this 21st century searching for such a theory.

His findings overthrew the clockwork-orderly-absolute-mechanistic-cause and effect-18th century-Newtonian science that had dominated Western thinking for over two centuries. His work laid the foundation for the development of the atom bomb and the Big Bang theory of creation. Quantum physics provides the underpinnings for major developments in semiconductors, television and lasers. Einstein's work also loosened scientists' and society's attachment to key assumptions about the order of the universe in science.

In particular, the ideas from quantum physics were popularized in thinking about modern social systems. Like Newtonian science before it, the new science also appealed to people trying to understand humanity and create better social systems. Newtonian social systems spawned beliefs in order, rationality, efficiency, cause-effect, control, etc. Post Einstein science brought forth a relativistic view—now morality, arts, politics, social relations were relative not absolute. And while Relativism, the idea that moral and ethical truths exist from the point of view of the beholder, was not an idea Einstein himself believed, relativism has become a popular social thought system.

Some of the people using quantum theory to understand how to improve communications began to focus working on communications theory focused not on the message, but on the garbage in between—the static. Others began thinking about dripping faucets, clouds, coastlines, and the formation of bubbles in water that was about to boil. People started to wonder if perhaps a study of turbulence and chaos would be relevant to such messy things as landslides, rush-hour traffic, epileptic seizures, and organizations going through traumatic change. The resulting Chaos Theory has hit its stride in the past decade as theorists begin to apply its insights to discontinuous, transforming change to a great many fields. Interestingly, while Einstein abhorred chaos and revolution for its own sake (living as he did in turbulent times—fleeing Nazi Germany, etc.) his work gave birth to Chaos Theory. And as a Chaos thought leader, he revolutionized our thinking and moved us out of the mechanistic Newtonian age into a relative range of possibilities we are just starting to explore.

CHAOS THEORY

Author, professor, and consultant Dr. Margaret (Meg) Wheatley has led the way in applying the insights of Chaos theory as well as other new scientific ideas to everyday organizational life in her book *Leadership and the new science*. In a paradoxical contradiction to conventional science, Dr. Wheatley reports that disorder can be the source of new order; and that dissipation—the loss of the old structure (embodied order)—is necessary to create new order. A self-organizing system releases its old form so it can reorganize in a form better suited to the demands of its changed environment. Living systems use information to decide whether, when and how to change—using the new information and energy of the dissipation to self-organize into a more complex form. Using this mental model, the things we fear in organizations—disruption, confusion, chaos, change—can all be reframed and reinterpreted not as signs of our eminent demise but rather as conditions required for creative growth. And the good news is that by studying weather patterns, scientists have noticed that while we cannot predict weather or wave patterns, over time we can see there is an invisible boundary, an order to those patterns—there is order without predictability. If Chaos theory is right for organizations, then, says Wheatley, order can emerge from chaotic change. The question she explores in her work and in her books is 'How?' What are the conditions that allow order to emerge from chaos? What do Chaos leaders do to make that happen?

Meg Wheatley on Leadership and the New Science

Chaos seems to be a critical part of the process by which living systems constantly re-create themselves in their environment. Strange attractors reveal the order that is inherent in certain kinds of chaotic systems. You can't see that order until you are able to watch the system evolve over a good period of time. When you look moment to moment at a system in chaos, all you see is chaos, total unpredictability. When you are able to watch the system develop over time, you can see the order that emerges out of the chaos. T.J. Cartwright, a planning expert, has given a definition of chaos that I love: "order without predictability."

Living systems, when confronted with change, have the capacity to fall apart so that they can reorganize themselves to be better adapted to their current environment. We always knew that things fell apart, we didn't know that organisms have the capacity to reorganize, to self-organize. We didn't know this until the

63

Noble-Prize-winning work of Ilya Prigogine in the late 1970's. But you can't self-organize, you can't transform, you can't get to bold new answers unless you are willing to move into that place of not-knowing which I call chaos. You get order through creating information and making it available.

The science of self-organizing systems says that if you want order you need a free flow of information, because information is what living systems use to transform themselves. In order to make sense of this information, an organization needs a strong core identity that is clear to everyone involved. An organization needs to know who it is in order to make sense of a chaotic environment. It needs filters that help people recognize information that is critical for the organization.

We need to have processes in which the whole organization is engaged in weaving its story. One of the lessons we can learn from the new science is that once you have formed a strong core identity you can then trust people to organize their own behavior around that identity, instead of organizing by policies and procedures. The behavior will look very different from person to person. And that will be okay, because (and this is one of the great lessons of chaos) you then stand back and look, not at those individual behaviors but at the pattern. Then you will be able to see the true pattern of the organization.

As managers and as consultants, we have always been interested in that big question: how do you motivate people. But the real answer is simple—you don't. Instead, you trust that they are self organizing systems who come with their own desire to thrive. They will make adjustments and do what is necessary for them to flourish.

In an organization, you don't have to "incentify" or motivate anybody. You have to create the conditions under which they can thrive, in which they are motivated. Among the things that human beings naturally seek are the ability to contribute and to make a difference, and the ability to be involved in satisfying social relationships. Those criteria show up at the top of every study I have ever looked at on why people work. If you design your organization around these criteria, it will have to be one in which people are not boxed into roles, in which they feel that they can continue to grow, learn, and develop, and in which a variety of relationships are available to them. When you box people in, when you see only a few of their attributes, you kill them. Once we've created organizations which really support people's contributions, then I don't think people are looking for complex rewards. I think they are looking for straightforward pay that feels fair. They are looking for pay that reflects their contribution (or their team's contribution) to the whole. Then allow them to be creative in solving the organizational problems.

What helps people be creative is experimentation—seeing what works by doing it. We need to create an atmosphere in which experimentation is welcome, and that means an atmosphere in which we don't take everything so incredibly seriously. We need to be much more forgiving, we need to be much more compassionate, we need to be in deeper relationships with one another. Play is a quality that leads to good experimentation. One plays by not killing people for making mistakes, and by going back to some vague memory that work should be fun, that when work is fun, it can still be very hard, but it has a whole different quality to it.

We already have a lot of examples of the principles that come from this new science at work in successful organizations. We just haven't had the language to talk about, and the lens to look at, what was making sense.

Chaos teaches us how to hang in the unknown and surrender. Perhaps this willingness to surrender to and create in the abyss is the source of charisma for some of the Chaos leaders.

Speaking of charisma, another very charismatic Chaos leader is Alexander the Great.

ALEXANDER THE GREAT

Alexander of Macedon (aka Alexander the Great), the only son of Philip of Macedon (359-336), had the best education (three years under Aristotle—the most renowned philosopher of his day) and the very finest education in warfare and politics. His daddy, who was the best known military strategist of the time, taught him. Philip left his son a mountain of gold, all of Greece, and a magnificent army. Of the three, the latter was the most crucial. Alexander's battles are marked by his ability to mix all the elements of his army and bring to bear just what was needed at just the right time.

Alexander himself was a bundle of contradictions and extremes. He was mystical and practical, a dreamer and a pragmatist. He was capable of planning grand strategies, yet paid attention to the details of supply and logistics while on the march. He paid careful attention to his image and it is very difficult for us to separate fact from propaganda. His soldiers adored him, as did most who met him. He was handsome, courageous, and intelligent. He was tireless in the field, able to out-work most everyone around him. Yet, he was also a dreamer, given to fits and moods. He had visions. His mother told him that he was not the son of Philip but the son of the God Apollo. In short, he was everything a legend should be. While we know Alexander did not conquer Asia by himself, he did exhibit tremendous personal bravery. He was always at the front and always in the thick of battle. Generals in pre-modern times usually led their men rather than commanding from behind as many generals do today.

Alexander never lost a battle. As the victories accumulated, his men came to believe that he was invincible. So did his enemies. Like other great generals, he knew and loved his men. He remembered their names and deeds, calling them by name when he would speak to them before a battle, citing their exploits. His veterans he sent home for a rest to Greece, allowing them to visit their families. He was liberal in his gifts and honors. All of these factors created an army that simply could not be stopped. Because its accomplishments so far eclipsed anything that had ever been done, Alexander and his Macedonians entered into legend.

Alexander set out in spring 334, after having had to re-settle affairs in Greece and Macedonia after his father's murder. One of the many puzzles about Alexander is whether he intended from the beginning to conquer the world. We know that he brought with him artists, geographers, historians, botanists, geologists and other scientists—something quite beyond the normal scope of a military expedition. Ever the politician, his first act was to visit Troy—the site of the great victory of the Greeks over Asia. The visit was also due to personal interest, for he greatly admired Homer and the heroes of the Trojan War. It was a brilliant propaganda gesture, and he followed it with astute diplomacy. As he marched down the Ionian coast, he liberated the Greek cities, restoring democracy, rather than conquering them. By posing as a liberator and savior, he won allies and gained many recruits here.

After winning his first big battle, Alexander rolled through Asia Minor, detouring to Gordium to meet up with his general Parmenio. Gordium was a town in Galatia, the ancient capital of the Phrygians. In the town was a wagon tied to a post. It was a very ordinary post and a very ordinary wagon with one exception: the yoke was fastened to the pole with a complex of knots so thoroughly tangled that it was impossible to unravel. The legend was that anyone who could loose the knot would be the conqueror of Asia. Alexander the Great naturally had to try his hand at this fabled knot, since he was in town anyway. He had announced his intention of conquering Asia, and to leave Gordium without testing the knot was unthinkable. So, he and some of his men, and a large crowd of locals, all made their way to the acropolis and the wagon.

The Gordian Knot was an especially difficult one in that there were no loose ends showing. Alexander tried for a while but was completely stumped. His attendants were concerned, for failure here would make poor propaganda. At last, Alexander cried out "What difference does it make how I loose it?" He pulled out his sword and cut the knot through. Thus did Alexander reveal that he was the one prophesied? It was a lovely play on words, for the Greek word was luein, which can mean "untie" but can also mean "sunder" or "resolve." From that story of Alexander came a phrase that is still used occasionally. To "cut the Gordian knot" means to slice through a problem that appears hopelessly complex by some simple, bold stroke.

While in Egypt, Alexander took another of his detours that became legendary. He visited the shrine of Zeus Ammon, a site sacred to Egyptians and Greeks alike. There, while visiting the Egyptian priests, he was proclaimed a god by the Egyptians—an honor he did not decline. He submitted to the Egyptian ceremonies, even going so far as to wear Egyptian dress. Alexander and his army accumulated a string of victories, culminating with the defeat of his nemesis, the Persian king Darius. Once Alexander became king of Persia, he began to adopt Persian dress, at least when dealing with Persian subjects. With his Macedonians, he still dressed as a Greek.

After solidifying his rule over Asia Minor, he announced his intention of conquering India in 327. None of the Greeks had ever encountered anything to prepare them for India. Alexander met serious resistance in India: the terrain, the monsoons, the fierce tribes, the long years of campaigning all combined to take some of the heart out of the Macedonians. He also encountered a really big guy with big elephants—the 7 foot tall Indian warrior-king named Porus. While Alexander eventually defeated Porus, killing the king's two sons and forcing Porus into an alliance, his men, encountering more and more resistance, eventually refused to go any further into India. It took them another year to fight their way back home.

Upon his return, Alexander entered into a frenzy of administrative activity. He took a Persian wife, and encouraged his officers to do likewise, arguing against traditional Greek parochialism. He had already founded many Greeks cities and now founded many more, giving land to his veterans. He instituted a common currency throughout his lands and he spoke of all his peoples being united under him.

Alexander was wounded in the neck and head at the Granicus River, in the thigh at Issus, and in the shoulder at Gaza. He suffered a broken leg in Turkestan, was wounded on three occasions in Afghanistan, and, most seriously, had his lung pierced by an arrow in India. Overworked, his wounds weakened him. He went on a boating trip while at Babylon, in summer, when the marshes of the river were full of fever. To add to all of this, he had engaged in another of his notorious drinking bouts the night before. Alexander the Great died of a fever 13 June 323. For four days there was silence in Babylon because people were in shock and mourning. His body was conveyed to Alexandria in Egypt, where it was buried. Though his first wife Roxane was pregnant with his first son, Alexander the Great left no heir.

As he lay dying, his comrades and generals came to him. Alexander had made no provision for his succession, for what reason we do not know. In any case, it now being clear that he would die, the issue had become pressing. They asked him the question that tormented them all. Who would get the empire? To whom would Alexander leave his conquests? His answer was eminently Greek and classic Alexander. He would leave his empire, he said, to the strongest.

Alexander was known as "The Great" even in his lifetime. Military experts still consider him one of the most outstanding commanders ever. Many explanations for this have been suggested: he suffered the same wounds as his soldiers, he paid attention to every single man in the army and he always led the attack in person. Some other reasons given for calling him Alexander the Great include:

- Charisma. Alexander was the only individual whose personal authority could hold his huge empire together. After his death it almost immediately fell apart into competing kingdoms. In 332 BC, in Egypt, the famous oracle of Siwa allegedly confirmed that Alexander had divine origins and that the god Zeus (Ammon) was his true father. We do not know how Alexander himself thought about his divinity, but it surely helped him to boost the myth around his person.

- World Shaper in a Changing World. Alexander ranks among figures like Jesus Christ and Napoleon in the category "individuals who shaped the world as we know it". Before Alexander, the region had been dominated by eastern cultures—Persians, Egyptians, and Babylonians. Alexander shifted the spotlight once and for all. From now on, the western societies of the Romans and the Greeks would take over the torch. Alexander started to mint the gold reserves of the Persian kings and used his resources to continue his conquests and to build new cities and ports. Greek civilization spread around the world, improving trade relations and economic activities. The economic system that began to take shape after Alexander's reign remained virtually unchanged until the Industrial Revolution of the 19th century.

- Administrative Effectiveness (expedient, occasionally brutal, and controversial). Alexander's empire was no rose garden. Especially after the final defeat of King Darius, the court was plagued by controversy and intrigue. Alexander had some of his loyal aides tortured and killed. Macedonians used brutal force to subdue the conquered peoples. Some reports say that they even butchered the sick and elderly. Alexander had 2,000 inhabitants mercilessly crucified. In modern Iran, he is still known as an evil king—a personification of the devil if you like—who did his very best to destroy the respectable old Persian culture and religion. On the other hand, some western scholars present Alexander as a visionary who believed in the peaceful co-existence of different nations and races within his empire. They refer—for example, to mass-weddings ordered by Alexander to reconcile Greeks and Persians.

One question frequently asked, and researched is "Was Alexander the Great gay?" Dr. Reames-Zimmerman, a classical scholar says "No!" not because he had no relationships with men and boys, particularly his beloved Hephaistion, but because our terms "homosexual" and "gay" are inappropriate terms for antiquity. Alexander's sexuality is more complex for several reasons.

- First, the general model for homoerotic attachments in antiquity was that of elder erastes (lover, pursuer, and active participant) and younger eromenos (beloved, pursued and passive participant). Individuals did not switch roles as the mood struck. Coeval partnerships were frowned on. Alexander and Hephaistion were coevals. This might mean some pressure against what we would assume to be, a homoerotic relationship.

- Second, the ancient Greeks generally thought who you slept with was a matter of personal choice, not a defining identity. Nonetheless, most scholars agree that Hephaistion's death hit Alexander hard. Alexander's grief is an indication of Hephaistion's significance to the conqueror. If Alexander is understood to be mourning a spouse (or spouse-equivalent), the severe nature of his mourning is comprehensible. Alexander's bereavement suggests that Hephaistion occupied the central emotional place in Alexander's life. Whatever the truth of their sexual involvement, their emotional attachment has never been seriously questioned.

- Third, the relationships between men and women in ancient Greece and Macedonia, particularly within the upper classes, differed radically from those of today. The polygamy of the Macedonian royal house would have been quite different even from that of a private family in the Greek south. So the fact that Alexander's primary emotional relationship might have been with another man is not only unsurprising, but perhaps predictable. Alexander had three wives (Roxane, Statiera, Parysatis) and perhaps two mistresses (Barsine, Pankaste/Kampaspe), and there is suggestion that he had occasional assignations as well. In his time and place, a liking for women need not be false in order for an equal liking for men to be true. As typical of his era, class and culture, Alexander seems to have been comfortably "bisexual."

- Finally, whatever one chooses to believe about Alexander's sexual relationship with Hephaistion, it would be reductive to characterize it solely in this way. Greek philia included a level of friendship that was particularly intense, one that is sometimes difficult for us now to grasp. Our models of friendship are not consonant with those of ancient Greeks where homoerotic desire was freely, sometimes emphatically, expressed. Intense friendship might well develop a sexual expression even while that expression was not the focus of the friendship, or even thought of as particularly characteristic of it. Alexander called Hephaistion Philalexandro, beloved friend of Alexander, which in his time expressed, in his own words, a deeper love than a sexual partner.

Alexander conquered and combined a number of disparate countries—being complexly ruthless and compassionate, dominating and conciliatory, open to exploring the world and its differences—definitely not easily categorized. His empire did not actually stay together after his death—no single person in his time was able to hold it together—but his lasting impact was the result of the churning of Greek-Macedonian culture with local cultures creating a more vibrant and long-lasting culture with aspects we still cherish today. Both the Greeks-Macedonians AND the conquered peoples were definitively changed as a result of both who he was and how the encounter with this Chaos leader Alexander the Great occurred. From what many, no doubt, experienced as chaos, a deep kind of cultural order—different but lasting—resulted.

MARGARET CHO

I'm not sure Margaret Cho would see herself as similar to people like Alexander the Great or Einstein, but in her own way she is also making a significant difference using a Chaos leadership style. What marks her style as Chaos is her intensity in busting conventional bubbles about who she is, what she can do and how she (and, by extension, many other Asian American women) should act.

Margaret Cho, a Korean American comedian sets out to destroy Asian stereotypes in the US but doesn't stop there. She also shoves people out of their comfort zones when it comes to family and sexual orientation issues. What also surprises people is that her raunchy stage persona is not necessarily the person you encounter in everyday interactions—again making it impossible for people to box her in.

She was born and raised in a very cutting-edge area of San Francisco, and started doing comedy when she was still in her teens. She says her biggest influence growing up was African American comedian Richard Pryor, "who had this very clear vision, which was that he would dare to reveal who he was at every opportunity. He never hid behind jokes. Even when he did characters, they were obviously real people. It was that honesty I always aspired to." Similarly Cho makes her relationship with her parents, and her social identity as Korean American, key parts of her act.

She won awards as a comedian, eventually landing the lead in a U.S. television situation comedy show called "All-American Girl". This show was supposed to be about the life of a single, Asian-American girl—herself. She was eventually told she was not 'ethnic enough', needed to tone her humor down, lose weight, and be more perky. This message "Play yourself but do not be yourself. Be our image of you" was very painful. Margaret Cho talks about how she risked her health—body and mind—trying to conform to their ideas and then wallowing in self-pity, alcohol and drugs when she inevitably failed. That painful experience is now part of her confessional show called *I'm the one that I want* in which she claims herself as a full-figured Asian American woman. "It's hard to be honest and vulnerable on stage…but what Richard Pryor and Roseanne Barr taught me was that there is strength and integrity in it." People respond to her strength, integrity, and vulnerability. Margaret Cho has found freedom by rejecting stereotypical labels while becoming a role model for many people who have similarly felt hemmed in by other people's preconceptions and resulting self-doubts.

This aspect of humanity—strength AND vulnerability—is a hallmark of the Chaos style leader. Cho knows she wants to influence people's thinking—to make the world a place where people can be themselves in full, unique, complex even controversial ways. Every time we encounter someone committed to being so fully authentic, even when it makes us uncomfortable in its content, it encourages each of us to believe that it is possible to offer ourselves as we are, and still make a significant difference. By causing us to question our cherished assumptions, and to break out of our comfortable boxes, Chaos style leaders like Margaret Cho offer us hopeful authenticity—rather than answers.

REFERENCES

CASE: Bayard Rustin
   FEATURE FILM: *Brother Outsider*. (2002). Public
      Broadcasting System.

   DOCUMENTARY: *You Don't Have to Ride Jim Crowe*.
      (1995). N.H. Public Broadcasting System.
CASE: Bill Clinton
   Clinton, B. (2004). *My Life*. Knopf.

CASE: Albert Einstein
   Einstein, A. (1993). *The World as I See It*. Citadel Press.

   Lightman, A. (1993). *Einstein's Dreams*. Warner Books.

RESEARCH REPORT: Leadership and the New Science.
   Wheatley, Margaret. (1992). *Leadership and the New
      Science*. Berrett-Koehler.

CASE: Alexander the Great

    Reames-Zimmerman, J. (Dissertation, 1998). *Hephaistion Amyntoros: Éminence Grise at the Court of Alexander the Great*. Pennsylvania State University: pp.152-179. See http://www.pothos.org/alexander/.

    Knox, E. L. (2004). History of Western Civilization course at http://history.boisestate.edu/westciv/alexander.

CASE: Margaret Cho

    Lawson, T. (August 21, 2002). "A New Cho Show on Film: Comedian Pushes the Limits on Family, Sex." *Detroit Free Press*.

    DVD: *The Notorious C.H.O.* (available in video stores.)

    DVD: *I'm the One that I Want*. (available in video stores.)

    Richardson, L. (March 19, 2001). "She's a Stand-up Academic for a Day: Comedian Margaret Cho Brings her One-Woman Act to a UCLA Class on Race Relations." *Los Angeles Times*.

Chapter 6
LYRICAL LEADERSHIP

Lyrical rhythm dancing is seen in the twirling, swirling, airy, light-on-your-toes, reach for the sky elegance associated with ballet. This style is deceptive because it looks far easier than it is. Its beauty emerges from the illusion of lightness and grace. Yet creating the impression that one is not limited by gravity requires incredible strength and balance. Ballet dancers spend countless hours in technique drills that are neither fun nor weightless. But when they reach the stage, we don't see the harsh practice; we marvel only at their soaring results. Roth uses words such as rope skipping, the acrobatic flight of a raven, aerial performers in the Cirque du Soleil, Balinese dancers, and the character Alice in the *Alice in Wonderland* story to evoke lyrical imagery. Another strong lyrical image is that of a duck floating serenely on top of the water, with its feet moving at hyper speed beneath its smoothly floating body.

Metaphorically, the lyrical rhythm re-presents how things are not quite what they seem. Things shift, change, look different depending on perspective—like if you were looking at the duck from above or below the water. Lyrical rhythm is about knowing things are always in process, becoming, changing—and that our so-called fixed reality is an illusion, a helpful even necessary illusion, but impermanent nonetheless. So folks who resonate to the lyrical rhythm are often willing to play with this—they know that 'this too will change' with time, a little push here, a little more attention there, a pull on that string and voilá—things are different

—and often we don't know how or why they changed, but they did. The puppet master was invisible to us.

As a leadership style, Lyrical tends to be more introverted and involving—you might call it more of a "pull" style if you were to contrast it with the more assertive "push" style of Staccato. The Lyrical leader is likely to encourage, engage, inquire, and empathize with others, drawing them out of their shells and/or into the Lyrical leader's orbit. Often these leaders exercise influence behind the scenes—for which they are sometimes acknowledged, sometimes not. These leaders might mentor people in the organization, using a light touch, but subtlety guide their protégés in ways that help the followers realize a potential they may have underestimated in themselves. And, often, like the ballet dancer, their work is invisible. A Lyrical leader's shape shifting may look like a person who is able to improvise, who thinks well on their feet, who adapts to new information and who responds to unexpected opportunities quickly. They are willing to stay with the process, in the energy of the moment, test it, and shift as needed. Lyrical leaders are often multitaskers—comfortable with doing many tasks at the same time.

DIANA, PRINCESS OF WALES

One example of the Lyrical style leader with grace with strength was Princess Diana. She was beloved, by many in part because she seemed fragile and vulnerable, in part because she was willing to poke fun at the ultra serious British Monarchy—including herself as a member, and in part because she was incredibly strong in her commitment to alleviating the suffering of those less fortunate than she. Her graciousness made it look easy. Yet we know, especially after her death, how much work and discipline went into that grace under pressure. When interviewed by the BBC and asked about how she coped with her new status as Princess of Wales, she described how she adapted and rose to the occasion.

"...Here was a situation which hadn't ever happened before in history, in the sense that the media were everywhere, and here was a fairy story that everybody wanted to work. And so it was, it was isolating, but it was also a situation when you couldn't indulge in feeling sorry for yourself; you had to either sink or swim. And you had to learn that very fast.... I swam. We went to Alice Springs, to Australia, and we went and did a walkabout, and I said to my husband: 'What do I do now?' And he said, 'Go over to the other side and speak to them.' I said, 'I can't, I just can't.' He said, 'Well you've got to do it.' And he went off and did his bit, and I went off and did my bit. It practically finished me off there and then, and I suddenly realized ... the impact. We had a six week tour ... and by the end,... I was a different person. I realized the sense of duty, the level of intensity of interest, and the demanding role I now found myself in."

This woman who was at the pinnacle of British, if not world society, and seen by many as the epitome of graciousness, described a very different inner experience.

"...I found myself being more and more involved with people who were rejected by society—with, I'd say, drug addicts, alcoholism, battered this, battered that—and I found an affinity there. And I respected very much the honesty I found on that level with the other people I met, because in hospices, for instance, when people are dying they're much more open and more vulnerable, and much more real than other people."

Even with the pressure from learning that Charles was having an affair she responded *"well, there were three of us in this marriage, so it was a bit crowded."* All the work in developing her core of strength as a leader became more evident at the time of the separation from Charles. Many expected her to go quietly off stage, underestimating her commitment to the causes she championed, and to influencing her sons' values as future royals. She was clear that...

> *"I'll fight to the end, because I believe that I have a role to fulfill and I've got two children to bring up...I am a free spirit—unfortunately for some... I've got my work that I choose to do, and I've got my boys, and I've got lots of opportunities... When I look at people in public life... I think the biggest disease this world suffers from in this day and age is the disease of people feeling unloved, and I know that I can give love for a minute, for half an hour, for a day, for a month, but I can give—I'm very happy to do that and I want to do that...I do things differently, because I don't go by a rule book, because I lead from the heart, not the head..."*

When she married the Prince of Wales she was the embodiment of the fairy tale princess. She matured over time, through finding and using inner strength that touched many. She role-modeled gracious resilience under pressure, and inspired many to continue working in-for the causes she championed. For many she is most remembered for her light touch, her willingness to share her heart and heartache with others who might not have her privileges yet, in some ways, shared her pain (and she theirs). She intended to make a positive difference in the world, and did so, in her Lyrical style.

Shift happens! Lyrical leaders help us understand that we may not have control over our lives but we do have power over how we deal with life's circumstances. Our maturity comes from learning that we co-create what we call our reality—that life is experienced subjectively—not just out there but in here—in the heart. Tapping into that experience determines the quality of our lives, making the subjective experience meaningful even if the objective length seems far too short—as many feel was the case for Diana, Princess of Wales.

SARGENT SHRIVER

A lot, if not most, people in the US have heard of the Peace Corps, the Special Olympics (celebrating abilities rather than disabilities), the War on Poverty that Lyndon Johnson launched, Volunteers in Service to America (VISTA) and Head Start. Many also know that George McGovern ran and lost his bid for the US Presidency with a Vice Presidential candidate. Who ties all those things together? A Lyrical style leader—Sargent Shriver.

Many people know Sargent Shriver was connected to the Kennedy's (he's married to Eunice), and that his daughter, Maria, is a newswoman and married to the current governor of California (Arnold Schwartzenegger), but few people know much about Sarge himself. Sargent Shriver, who was committed to humanitarian causes and worked tirelessly all his life to see life improve for the poor, people with disabilities, and people of color, never won an election, was often seen as a hanger-on to the Kennedys and a 'lightweight, limousine liberal' who capitalized on his connections, good looks, and celebrity aura.

But Sargent Shriver's biographers assert that he took vague policy directives to deal with issues of poverty and turned them into programs that are still making a positive difference for the poor and disenfranchised today. He served as the first director of the Peace Corps that he helped design, headed the War on Poverty despite worries that it would risk his relationship to the Kennedys, created the Special Olympics, and was George McGovern's Vice Presidential running mate in 1972. He had a knack for energizing and then directing the energy of young people towards making a positive difference for themselves and the world—changing millions of lives for the better through the programs he's championed and run. Pretty good legacy for someone called a lightweight. It is not uncommon for people with the Lyrical style to be underestimated in their commitment to accomplishing their goals, especially since they often work to achieve those goals with or through other people, as Sarge did.

While Sargent Shriver never looked like the authoritative leader many people expect in positions of power, he did hold positions of 'leadership' at various times in his career. In our next example, the leader doesn't resemble most people's idea of a leader at all. Spider Old Woman is actually a character from tales of the Hopi, a Native American tribe in the Southwest US.

HOPI SPIDER WOMAN

"The Races at Tsikuvi" is a Hopi tale in which Spider Old Woman helps her protégé win a race against a neighboring village. At stake was the future of both villages, a challenge between different styles of leadership, and a lesson about valuing the best performers and all contributors in a village. As background information, it is helpful to know that the Hopi culture is matrilineal. The oldest woman of the clan has enormous social power. The clan owns all the land, and the clan is defined by this woman and her female blood relations. The clan leader in this society is expected to be good, wise, loving, respectful, and maintain harmony within the village.

There were two villages, both with chiefs. In Tsikuvi the men and boys were fast runners and proud of it. In the smaller village of Payupki, there was only one fast male runner. The Payupki boy watched the others run, saw he could run faster than all of them, and told the chief of his village. The proud chief of the Tsikuvi village eventually came to challenge the chief of the Payupki village to a race. The Tsikuvi chief went back to his village and plotted to win the races unfairly. Their village elder, Spider grandmother, came down to council with her bag of herbs. The men of the village were not respectful of her, shoved her, and told her they didn't want her. She took her bags and left, going over to the Payupki village. She was warmly welcomed and respected in that village. She told them that the men of the Tsikuvi village were plotting to win the races unfairly, but that she would help their Payupki racer. She rubbed herbs and medicines on his legs and told him to rest, knowing that the men of the Tsikuvi village would be up all night plotting and gloating over their anticipated victory.

The first set of races were a rude surprise for Tsikuvi. They lost all they bet. The Payuki enjoyed their winnings and shared them with Spider grandmother as they celebrated together. They knew there would be a rematch and told the boy to start preparing. The boy started his training but his sister, watching him run, thought he was not very fast. They did a series of training races where she gave him a head start, raced him, beat him, and returned to her chores before he finished his part of the race. It eventually became clear to him that she was a far faster runner. He told this to the chief and the village decided that she would be their representative. When the Payupki chief declared that a girl would be their runner the Tsikuvi chief scoffed, "it's OK if that's all you have". The Tsikuvi bet every thing they had from their village on winning the races, including all their women. Spider grandmother, not only put herbal medicines on the Payupki girl runner, but turned herself into a small spider and whispered in her ear what she must do to avoid the tricks of the Tsikuvi tribe and its runner. The girl was running when the other runner turned himself into a dove and passed her. Spider woman signaled to her bird, the hawk, to knock the dove out of the air. They did that four times. Then spider woman knew they would do something different. She said "when I tell you to jump (left-right-up), you must jump quickly." The girl kept running but jumped when the spider told her to jump, without question, and each time something landed right where she had been. With Spider woman's help the girl won the race, and the village won all the Tsikuvi's women. The Tsikuvi did not care about losing the women, thinking they could do women's work that looked easy to them. Eventually they learned they could not, but it was too late. The women lived in the Payupki village and were treated so well they were happy to stay, and Spider woman helped the now larger village stay together—defeating the overly proud yet disrespectful Tsikuvi a third time.

Hopi Spider Old Woman does not present the typical image of a leader—but the story illuminates a few points that are important for understanding the Lyrical style, and circumstances that contribute to effectiveness when using the lyrical approach to leadership. First of all, she is not what she seems on the surface, which the Tsikuvi's learned the hard way. In this story, she's a literal shapeshifter, as well as a shaman, trainer, wise woman, guide, and mentor. She does not attempt to run the race for the Payupki, but she is willing to share wisdom, to mentor and to guide the runners before and during the race. Lyrical style leaders often serve as guides or mentors to others. Secondly, Hopi Spider Old Woman leaves the tribe that disrespects her and does not want her help, and serves the tribe that does. In many traditions, it is believed that people develop best when they have become teachable—that is when followers are open and willing to listen and learn from people who may know more than they do about certain matters. "When the student is ready, the teacher appears". Lyrical style leaders often know how and when to support the growth and direction of people who may be called to act. Not all leaders are the doers themselves—some of us make a positive difference in the world, as Hopi Spider Woman did, by removing obstacles and supporting the action of others.

DOUG PATTERSON

A person who exemplifies this style in daily life is Doug Patterson. Doug is committed to helping people of color articulate, develop and contribute their best to organizations of all kinds. He is not particularly interested in working as a leader or manager in any specific corporation or organization. Nor does he have a passion for teaching. But he knows lots of people who do—working as leaders and managers of organizations and/or have a passion for teaching topics that help people be more effective at work. His contribution, as he sees it, is to maintain relationships with those people, and to inspire-encourage-support them as they contribute resources, time, energy, and talents to a range of developmental programs for people of color.

Doug does this behind the scenes work without benefit of a lofty title, but with the respect of people who know of his unflagging commitment and incredible competence in finding resources and eliminating barriers to this work. Doug is a Lyrical leader making a positive difference through others. He is fully comfortable working behind the scenes. And he started doing this work when he was in the lowest ranking position in his organization. What he realized is that with passionate commitment and the right network he could influence people, even if he did not have formal authority or position power. This is a lesson many Lyrical style leaders teach us.

INVISIBLE WORK

In my research with a team of people looking at gender equity in organizations, we noticed a tendency for some female leaders to use the Lyrical style. They do a great deal of mostly invisible, behind-the-scenes work in order to short-circuit problems, while maintaining a veneer of serenity and graciousness. Ironically, however, since these women manage to avoid catastrophes, they rarely receive recognition or reward for having solved problems…since those problems never occurred in the first place! The invisible work was also often invisible to them, their co-workers, their peers, as well as their bosses. The challenge with the Lyrical style is to get everyone to acknowledge and appreciate the work that goes into making this leadership look effortless.

As Joyce Fletcher writes in her books and articles on invisible work and relational practice, the skills that it takes to make teams work, people collaborate, and have shared learning-problem solving in organizations are often devalued and/or made invisible for several reasons.

- First, the skill set is usually not seen as a SKILL set, but rather individual traits or characteristics. If we think a person is born with the ability to work well with others we (and they) often take that ability for granted. As a result, that person's efforts in developing their competence may not be evident, nor will other people think that they too can develop those competencies.

- Second, relationship skills are often undervalued in many cases because it is hard to quantify their contribution to results. In many organizations we don't value what we cannot count. So relationship skills literally don't count.

- Third, despite our rhetoric that we value collaboration, teamwork and systemic thinking, we reward individual achievement, heroic efforts, autonomy, and specialization. And it is folly to hope for A (collaboration, teamwork and systemic thinking), while rewarding B (individual achievement, autonomy and specialization).

- Fourth, we often misunderstand people involved in relational practice—thinking they are just being 'nice' rather than competent and committed to outcomes. Or we think that they are hiding behind others when they talk about 'we' because they're afraid to take credit for personal achievements, and that they are weaker than big-bold-strong leaders who stand out front.

I talk about invisible work and women, because there is significant and robust research that attests to women being in this situation far too frequently. This does not mean that it never happens that men doing relational work find themselves in situations where their contribution to making shared goals happen is undervalued. Whether you are female or male doing devalued invisible work that influences people to work respectfully towards a shared goal, Fletcher's work can provide a way to understand the dynamics of that devaluation. I admit to wanting to include the Lyrical style, especially with its risk of invisibility, as a leadership style in this book in order to help more people see how important their contribution is and to encourage us all to acknowledge these contributions. If you resonate to the lyrical rhythm, and recognize yourself as someone using this leadership style, and you would like to be acknowledged for your work, we suggest you:

- name your relational skills as skills, not as traits.

- claim your accomplishments using these skills (by putting them on your performance appraisals, for instance),

- measure your contributions as a result of using these skills. When you make them count, others are more likely to value these skills.

SANDRA CHARLES

Sandra worked for a publishing company in an administrative capacity. Everyone in the organization called her the 'glue' that kept things together. She was a master at managing all the tasks, big and small, required to keep things running smoothly—negotiating with authors and printers, solving problems with co-workers and vendors, smoothing ruffled feathers with clients, and members of the board of directors, mediating conflicts between people at all levels up-down-and-sideways in the organization—and doing all of this in addition to her 'own work' as art director for their publications. After years of working in this organization that many described as a big family, she felt burnt out and unappreciated. She was not exactly sure why. She was acknowledged as an important member of the team and for her official work. But she really had no clue about how much other, relational, work she was doing. And no one in the organization really understood the value of that work until she left. It took her some time and lots of reflection to start to see that her 'natural abilities' to work well with people, negotiate, and solve conflicts were skills that she was using. These skills took real energy, and provided value to that organization. She has since been able to capitalize on those skills as an independent consultant, and been able to explicitly influence people at her former organization once she saw what she did as leading—just in a different way—a Lyrical way.

I was in a bookstore recently and saw a new book on the stands called "*Founding Mothers*" by Cokie Roberts. The jacket says this book is about the women who were partnered with the founding fathers. These women organized social events at which the men, even those who did not like each other, were made to behave in a civil way to each other. Cokie Roberts asserts that their invisible work, these 'good women behind the men' made a significant difference for us all because, without their intervention, the men would not have been able to resolve their differences enough to enact their shared interest in the founding of the United States.

It's not news to notice that a lot of invisible work goes on, or to note that relational work is undervalued. What is news for many people is to consider the relational skills used in what we've called invisible work as a leadership style—a way of making a significant difference that is just as important and as valuable as the other styles of leading with which we are more familiar.

Dee Koh, when she was a student in one of my leadership classes, provided a beautiful description of a Lyrical leader.

You are a leader when your heart sketches the outline for a mural and people line up to help you paint.

As Dee talked about this definition she described a vision that was not driven by money or the need for external power, but rather by integrity. The sketch is from her heart and the leader has such quality relationships with people that they joyfully join her in manifesting that heart-held vision. The process of painting the mural is shared—which is its own joy—and the final mural is the co-creation of leader and followers. Even after the leader is gone the mural remains as a legacy to their collective creation.

REFERENCES

CASE: Diana, Princess of Wales
      Buskin, Richard. (1997). *Princess Diana: Her Life Story 1961-1997*. Consumer Guide Books.

CASE: Sargent Shriver
      Stossel, S. & Moyers, B. (2004). *Sarge: The Life and Times of Sargent Shriver*. Smithsonian Institution Press.

CASE: Hopi Spider Woman
      Spider Old Woman: Tales From the Hopi. (1994). Leadership case published by Hartwick Humanities in Management Institute at Hartwick College. Oneonta, N.Y.

      Courlander, H., transcriber. (1982). *Hopi Voices: Recollections, Traditions and Narratives of the Hopi Indians*. Albuquerque University.

CLIENT: Doug Patterson
All client examples are provided by real people whose names have
been changed for confidentiality reasons.

RESEARCH REPORT: Invisible Work
        Fletcher, J. (March, 2001). "Invisible Work: The
            Disappearing of Relational Practice at Work."
            Simmons College Center for Gender in
            Organizations.

CLIENT: Sandra Charles
All client examples are provided by real people whose names have
been changed for confidentiality reasons.

Roberts, Cokie. (2004). *Founding Mothers: The Women Who
        Raised Our Nation.* William Morrow.

Chapter 7
STILLNESS LEADERSHIP

The essential stillness rhythm would be silence. Stillness in dance may often look like no movement. If there is movement, it is slow and so disciplined, grounded, and centered that the movement itself is a healing process. Roth says the energy of stillness is focused on the inner dance where each movement rises from the ocean of being. In dance, stillness energy originates in the center of the body and the center makes the abdomen rise and fall. Or maybe energy directed through the arms causes a ripple in the fingertips. Stillness could be the kundalini energy that travels up the spine that makes you rebalance your head so it takes no effort to hold it upright simultaneously recharging your whole physical system. It's the breath, the slow taking in and giving out of energy that nourishes body and soul. We can live without food for weeks and without water for a few days, but we cannot live without breathing for more than a few minutes. In the stillness, we know the power of the breath, the essence of life in the oxygen consumed.

Other words associated with stillness rhythm include jelly fish, a cloistered convent, a shadow, a cracked mask, Kali Ma, Buddha, a coiled snake, breath meditation—insight meditation. In art, think of the still life paintings of Georgia O'Keefe; in architecture, the Acropolis in Athens. Metaphorically, stillness is a deep understanding of the in and the out, the light and the shadow, the head and the heart—all opposites actually contained in unity. The rhythmic energy flow is bounded, directed, grounded, and expressed with intention, compassion and detachment.

Stillness leaders know how to use silence, how to be still enough to listen to what is going on in their organizations so that they are connected to its raison d'etre—its very life purpose. They are often willing and able to listen at multiple levels—to listen to the surface statements and to listen to the deeper intentions we try to communicate.

LISTENING

In the Chinese character for "To Listen" there are strokes that symbolize heart-mind, ear, undivided attention, and eyes. Listening starts with keeping your ears open, leaving your heart open, giving the gift of your undivided attention, not thinking about what you want to say until it's your turn to talk, making eye contact, and keeping your mouth completely shut—until the person talking has completed their comment. When they have finished, it is effective then to check whether you understood what they said, and whether they think you understood what they said. To do this, paraphrase what they said and/or ask open-ended clarifying questions. After it is agreed that one person has communicated, it is then acceptable for the other person to share his/her perspective—speaking from their own experience, not reinterpreting the first speakers' ideas.

Listening, as described above,

- demonstrates respect for the other person,
- allows us to entertain the possibility that all people's behavior makes sense from their perspective,
- is often the gateway to acknowledging, understanding, and maybe eventual agreement with various perspectives,

- allows us to potentially uncover shared interests below colliding positions
- helps us gain the confidence that the differences between us need not hinder our ability to work towards the things we agree upon.

Many people say that deep listening with rapt attention from a Stillness leader can feel both incredibly personal-transformative and impersonal-distanced at the same time—like they see into your heart-head, evoke your potential, yet direct you towards doing something bigger than that which serves your personal ego.

Stillness leaders value reciprocity—the taking in and giving out—with employees, suppliers, customers and community. This reciprocity is a reflection that us vs. them is usually dysfunctional when what you are seeking is a shared goal. Stillness leaders work with light and shadow, seeing them as aspects of the same energy, They might guide us to and through those parts of ourselves we are most likely to ignore or deny. They help us know our whole selves—light and shadow, perhaps show us how not to project our shadow onto others (usually 'them' of the us vs. them). Many Stillness leaders help us see not just our own personal shadows and the consequences of rejecting-projecting that onto individual others—but also to look at the collective-rejected-projected shadow that blocks many more enlightened human efforts to create social equity.

Stillness leaders seem to be evident and effective in situations that call for values/belief changes. There is something about their ability to tap into our deeper, shared desires that allows them to get below the surface disagreements and bring our places of shared value to light. The Stillness leadership style has been used in many modern social justice and civil rights movements. Millions of people have benefited from the being-power of Mahatma Gandhi, and the leaders who've followed his example.

93

MAHANDAS K. GANDHI

A small brown thin-legged man, often shown in homespun white cloth, who had not been elected to any office and represented no government is credited with ending British colonial rule in India using a non-violent approach. Millions of people in India followed him. Moreover, his example has been used successfully in civil and human rights campaigns around the world ever since. Mohandas (Mahatma) Gandhi is an example of the potential in the Stillness leadership style. "Strength does not come from physical capacity. It comes from an indomitable will". His indomitable will came from having his actions grounded in three core principles—ahimsa, satyagraha, and karma yoga.

- Ahimsa has been called active compassion. As a spiritual principle, it represents the love that remains when all thoughts of violence against anything living are dispelled.

- Satyagraha is often called truth-force. In practice, it means to hold firmly to the deepest truth and that you tap a kind of soul force that enables you to stand firm for what you believe in. It is a spiritual rather than religious principle. In many ways Gandhi did not think any particular religious practice had a monopoly on the truth. He sought God, not orthodoxy and was spiritually eclectic. In his daily spiritual practice he was likely to mix Hindu venerations, with Buddhist chants, readings from the Koran, Zoroastran verses, and sing Christian hymns.

- Karma yoga in practice is an understanding of work as a path or vehicle for expressing and getting to enlightenment. Gandhi is known for keeping his hands busy, making the cloth that he is seen wearing in most photos. This cloth making served many uses—the process was a kind of stillness meditation. Also, he encouraged other Indians to spin, knowing that by doing so, Indians might gain some independence from foreign, especially British cloth. In the process Indians learned a manual labor skill and felt better about themselves by making something tangible and useful with their own hands. This was important for people who had lost their self respect during the long period of colonial rule. It also worked for Gandhi because he felt that mechanization and materialism could sicken the human spirit.

By acting from these three spiritual principles and combining them with non-cooperation, Gandhi embodied a spirit-based, still, steadfast power that changed the world. He is often quoted as saying we must "Be the change we want to see in the world." He is a clear example of human-being-power.

While Gandhi was clear about what he was willing to live and die for, he was also clear that he was unwilling to kill for any reason. "An eye for an eye will make the whole world go blind," he said. Yet his version of non-violence was not passive, but rather the active living out these principles in every situation for every kind of person—even his so-called enemies. Gandhi's deep sense of political purpose was grounded in his everyday life. He was not a saint, nor was he perfect—as he himself admitted. He regularly dealt with his own shadow, and his own negative impulses. He is reported to have neglected and even humiliated his wife Kasturba most of his life. And yet his willingness to use silence, stillness, to hold fast, to confront—if not master his own shadow—and to be the change he wanted to see in the world, impressed the British, inspired his followers in India to resist oppression and create a free state, and provided the example many leaders and non-violent resistors have used world wide to make the world more civil.

Gandhi was the role model for Martin Luther King, Jr. as he led the non-violent movement for African-American civil rights, the British suffragist Emmeline Pankhurst's hunger strikes in support of voting rights for women, Gays and Lesbians at the Greenwich Village New York Stonewall Inn resisting a police raid, the nameless man in Tiananmen Square seeking democratic voice in China, the founder of the Solidarity labor union and eventual president of Poland Lech Walesa leading his fellow Polish workers, American students protesting the Vietnam War burning draft cards, the Tibetan Dalai Lama working for de-occupation of his country, the organizers of the United Farm Workers Cesar Chavez and Dolores Huerta, and Myanmar-Burma Nobel-peace-prize winner under house arrest Aung San Suu Kyi...plus all the people who led in less visible ways in all of these movements.

TRANSFORMATIONAL LEADERSHIP

Gandhi and the many that followed his example are often cited as examples of transformational leaders. Transformational leaders motivate people to transcend self-interest and self-imposed limits for a greater collective vision. The transformational leader raises the level of awareness, level of follower consciousness about the significance and value of designated outcomes, and increases follower's sense of their being viable ways of reaching shared goals. Transformational leaders get people to transcend their own self-interest for the sake of the team, the organization or society. They are called transformational leaders because, by focusing on follower needs and input, they empower followers to become leaders themselves—in short they transform followers into leaders. Stillness leaders help their followers tap into that powerful transformative motivation that can only come from within.

REFERENCES

CASE: Mahandas K. Gandhi
Fischer, L. (1950). *The Life of Mahatma Gandhi*. Harper Collins Publishers.

Gandhi, Mahatma. (1994). Leadership case published by the Hartwick Humanities in Management Institute at Hartwick College. Oneonta, N.Y.

RESEARCH REPORT: Transformational Leadership
Bass, B. M. (1985). *Leadership and Performance Beyond Expectations*. Free Press.

Avolio, B., & Bass, B. M.; edited by Hunt, J.G., Baliga, B. R., Dachler, H.P., & Schriesheim, C.A. (1987). *Transformational Leadership, Charisma and Beyond in Emerging Leadership Vistas*, pp. 29-50. Heath.

Chapter 8
BORN? MADE? CALLED?

In the beginning of this book I mentioned that we are often trying to figure out if leaders are born with characteristics and traits that destine them to become leaders. Or if they learn leadership through their life experiences as they master skills necessary to influence others. Or if they are people who are in the right place at the right time and therefore able to make a significant difference because of situational factors.

Born? What's your style? Your Pattern?

The five rhythms described in previous chapters address the 'born' aspect of leadership. Implied in each description is the notion that we resonate to certain rhythms, if not from birth certainly from such a young age and core place that our response feels almost innate. What I did not talk about in those chapters is what to do if you have more than one rhythmic resonance. And when I talk about this subject, people also usually want to know if there are better or worse ways to lead or if they should resonate to all the rhythms. I will address those issues in this chapter.

Made? How can you develop style skills?

The second stream of thought has to do with how leaders develop their skills. Whether you have clarity about your rhythmic resonance or not, you can learn to use important leadership skills that I will describe under 'Developing Your Leadership' in this chapter. I've organized the skills by rhythm to stay consistent with the Dance of Leadership metaphor—but all of the skills can be useful in the right circumstances—and as skills, all of them are learnable. There are certainly more leadership skills than those I cover in this chapter. The samples I provide here are intended to have you think of some skills you might not yet use, or maybe did not think to use as *leadership* skills. Skill development only occurs with practice. I'll describe the skills but you have to take the time to try them, either in classes or with friends and colleagues, I hope you will become competent using them.

Called? In which situation each style effective?

In the last part of this chapter I will summarize some of the situations that seem to call for skills and abilities from each of the styles.

RHYTHMIC PATTERNS – THE WAVE

Gabrielle Roth's original idea behind the rhythms came from her observation that much of life's energy moves as a wave—and she named that wave flowing-staccato-chaos-lyrical-stillness-flowing… In other words life energy moves in different ways through all the rhythms. In using this material with people as they claim their leadership resonance, I notice a range of responses. The rhythms are a typology—a way to characterize people so that we can understand them better and be more patient with people who are not like us. Like any typology, we find people who clearly represent the various types, we find people who blend one or two types, and we find people who don't seem to fit into any of the types. My intent in the Dance of Leadership is not to box you into a type—but to broaden our conception of who leads and how leadership happens. If you find yourself clearly represented in one or two of the rhythmic descriptions, yeah! If you can identify one of two rhythms you really dislike—that's

100

good too, since you now know what does not move you. If you read about the rhythms and can feel them all, perhaps recognize that each one can be effective in certain situations, then skip down to the next part of this chapter if you want to—since you're getting ahead of me.

Distinguishing the types

Many people follow the Staccato leader precisely because they project a strong sense of being in control. The Staccato leader is good at shaping energy. Flowing leaders are appreciated because they seem so grounded, so 'in the flow' (and thus still in control). The Flowing leader is in the comfort zone—the comfort zone being that place where one knows what to do and can do what needs doing. The Staccato leader creates the comfort zone—letting us know what to do and/or how to do it. The Chaos leader is in the freak-out zone—knowing neither what to do nor how to do it—but trying to move to a learning zone where they will know either what to do or how to do it.

Flowing leaders are sensitive to the flow of their energy, follow it, and stay true to it. They ground that energy in collective values. Staccato leaders organize our energy, focus and direct it. Chaos leaders dive below the surface, logical mind to the intuitive mind; Lyrical leaders integrate the spontaneous, poetic intelligence with the logical intelligence and adapt their actions to the needs of the situation at that moment. Chaos, Lyrical and Stillness leaders all know how much we try to hold our lives together, to keep everything secure and predictable, but each of those three styles knows that life is not orderly and predictable. Chaos leaders say surrender to that unpredictability and trust that order will emerge. Lyrical leaders say adapt your responses to the needs of the moment and keep as many balls in the air through multitasking as you can. Stillness says integrate the light and shadow; be that which you want, give that which you want to receive.

Staccato and Flowing are both extraverted leadership styles. Chaos has both an introverted and extraverted expression. Lyrical and Stillness are introverted styles. Men and women express all five styles. There is no best style for either gender. However, at the archetypal level, Roth would call Flowing a feminine style and Staccato a masculine style. Chaos is when the Flowing and Staccato meet and clash, and Lyrical would be the result of the Flowing-Staccato integration in an effective way.

I must say though, in my work with many leaders, people tend to find one or two of the styles they like, and at least one where they have a fairly negative reaction. Most people can't really feel all of them the same way. That doesn't mean that they can't use the skills from those styles—just as we can dance to any kind of music—we just don't always want to do that. So, no need to feel any strong push to become adept at using all the styles. If it moves you, great! If it doesn't—let it go. At least for now.

And no—there is not one style that is intrinsically better than the others. Our society and many of the people I work with will come into my session with a preconceived notion about which style is best, *in general*, and that is based less on their own authentic resonance than on media generated-culturally accepted norms about leading and leadership. In our society, leadership and Staccato style are nearly synonymous. The people listed under Stillness are venerated, but often seen as idealistic martyrs—and not usually the role model for everyday leadership. Flowing style leaders can sometimes be acknowledged, and when we must have chaos, we're grateful for people comfortable enough to lead through that style. But we usually do not really like to be around leaders who cause chaos too much—the frame busters—because they make us uncomfortable. Many of the Stillness leaders make people uncomfortable—mostly because they force us to look at our individual and collective shadows. And Lyrical is often not seen as leadership at all. But those are the ideas you had before you started reading the Dance of Leadership. By now, you know I'm not suggesting that any style is better or worse than another.

DEVELOPING YOUR LEADERSHIP

FLOWING*: Using Aikido to see conflict as a dance of energy*. Aikido is a defensive Japanese martial art that teaches a wonderful methodology for channeling aggressive energy into either productive channels or harmless ones, without taking you off center. Thomas Crum and James Clawson have both described the basics of this approach. First of all, you must center yourself.

Centering is a special mind-body state you can learn in most martial arts (or even stress reduction) classes. From a centered place, your awareness is heightened and your ability to concentrate is increased. It makes you response-able. You are ready to respond to whatever comes your way. Thomas Crum says one reason Michael Jordon would get the ball so often in the final minute of play is that he had consistently demonstrated his ability to stay centered under pressure. While many of us think his abilities are extraordinary, ordinary people can and do center all the time. You've probably done it many times when you were in flow—when you were playing as a child, doing something you really enjoyed, intensely concentrating on some activity or person who mattered to you. That's centering. It's a skill—and like any skill, practice improves it.

You can experience the power of centering through a series of exercises that demonstrate key principles physically. You'll need a partner for this. Stand stable. Stand up straight so that you cannot be pushed over by your buddy. Most people get a bit rigid or lean forward. (No shoving please). Now imagine that you are centering all of your energy in the point right near your navel, that your energy is grounded down through your feet (move your toes so you feel the ground). Take a couple of deep breaths, remembering to fully release the air from your lungs. Keep relaxed eye contact with your buddy while you relaxedly stand stable.

Most people now notice an appreciable difference in their ability to stand stable. Think positive thoughts. You did it. You centered.

Now think of what could go wrong. Think of anything stressful. Your ability to stand stable will evaporate. This demonstrates the power of positive and negative thinking on your ability to stay centered. This is just one of many exercises you can read about, learn, and practice using Aikido techniques. One of my favorites is the energy arm. In this exercise, we demonstrate how rigid resistance takes more energy than going with the flow—for the same result. But to experience that, you'll have to take a class. It's not one to try on your own.

From a centered place you enhance your ability to respond to anything that comes at you. This is particularly helpful in conflict situations where you may have aggressive mental energy coming your way. We all know that conflict is a fact of life. Aikido teaches both physical and mental centering. You need physical centering to handle physical aggression. Ki, the middle part of the word Aikido, means energy. Aikido means "the way of harmony with energy". The Aikido approach to physical aggression then is not to meet force with force, but rather to harmonize with the energy from the aggressor, and then redirect that so it does not harm you, move you, or harm the aggressor. At the mental level, when a person's mental approach in a conflict is win-lose, from a centered place you are more likely to be able to channel that energy into a win-win or win-neutral result.

Most of us think strength comes from being rigidly strong. "When the going gets tough, the tough get rigid." In the Flowing style, power is energy flowing freely toward a purpose. This is in contrast to the Staccato approach that would be to meet force with force. To stay in the flow you must not be tense, and your weight-center of gravity is not in the upper part of your body. When we are stressed we tend to hold our breath bringing the center of gravity upwards. Aikido teaches you to keep your energy weight

104

lower, to ground it, to relax but be ready to move when it's necessary.

Most of us dread conflict. Aikido teaches us that conflict can be a dance of energy—an opportunity we embrace when we know how to channel that energy into productive directions.

STACCATO: *Goal Setting.* Staccato is about action. Not just any action, the right action. Goal setting skills really help us decide what we want, why we want it, and what motivates us to take the actions that will get us there. Since we are working on your leadership development, this goal setting exercise will be for you as an individual. The principles of goal setting also apply when you are leading others—and you can make goals for a team, for a department, for an organization, for our society. But for now, let's start with you.

You'll need several sheets of blank paper, something to write with, a timer and some quiet time. I suggest that once you start answering a question, you just keep your hand moving. Write rapidly, time your writing and don't think too much. It's also usually better to actually write rather than type—for some reason the hand writing connects to the brain-heart energy differently than when we type. But writing or typing is up to you in the end. This is a kind of individual brainstorming session in the beginning. Too much thinking may block creativity. This exercise starts with flow and gets structured by staccato. In the beginning, I want you to get to what really matters to you, get that out of you and down on paper. We're not concerned with "How" right now, but I will ask you to write down why these goals are important to you. The 'why' invokes and explains your motivation.

You can make goals for any part of your life—Personal Development, Things, Finances, Relationships, Work. Let's have you practice the goal setting process by starting with personal development goals. Personal development goals can be about any area of life. Who would you like to become? How would you like to express the true you? What skills, ability, character traits, and values do you want to make evident in all of your work and life? What do you want to accomplish with your career? Be creative, outrageous, it's your life. Consider anything you want to do or be in the next 1-20 years.

Brainstorm a list of personal development goals for 3 minutes starting now. Keep writing down anything that comes to mind. Do the next step only after you've done this one.

1. Now look at the list of personal development goals you made. Put a 1 next to any goal you think you can achieve in 1 year or less. Put a 3 next to a goal you could do in 3 years or less. Continue for 5, 10 and 20 years.

2. Select the three important goals you'd like to achieve within the next year. Select the top three based on either urgency or importance TO YOU, not because they are important to someone else. These are your goals.

3. Write three paragraphs, one for each of those goals, about "why" that goal is important to you. Give yourself a total of 6 minutes to write the paragraphs—2 minutes for each.

4. Now let's start structuring the goals. Goals motivate us most when they are S.M.A.R.T.: Specific, Measurable, Attainable, Result-Oriented, and Time-Bound. Look at the three goals you selected. You now know what they are and why you want them. Now take each goal and define it more specifically. How will you know when you have achieved the goal? How will you keep track of your progress towards the goal? What is the result you want to experience when you have achieved the goal? How long do you think it will take you to achieve it? It is better to have a series of moderate goals than a couple of big, hairy,

audacious goals. We know from research with high achievers that successful attainment of moderate goals results in greater achievements in the long run. So don't overdo it. Make your goals reasonable.

5. Select one activity you can do in the next 48 hours—a single action you can take right away—that would be a step towards attaining any one of these goals. After every goal setting session take some action that moves you toward your goal right away—otherwise you lose energy and momentum. Your action should also be a S.M.A.R.T. action, and one that is completely within your control.

For example, suppose you really value learning—and you've put off learning the computer for years because you've been so busy with other things in your life. You're actually a bit computer phobic and embarrassed because even your kids can handle computers well. So one of your goals is refined to 'become more comfortable with computer technology' so you can join the 21st century, communicate with friends and family via email, have more job options at work, and put up your own website.

To be more specific, you might say what you want to learn on the computer. So let's say you want to buy your own computer, take a basic internet navigation course, and learn Dream Weaver. Now 'become more comfortable with the computer' is specific. You have three things to do that you will be able to know if you've done them. So the results are measurable and you can even tick off each of those things as you complete them. We still won't know if you are more 'comfortable' with the computer, but we know you'll have one and be using it. Comfort is a feeling. It's likely you will be more comfortable if you're more skilled. With goal setting though we focus on actions, behaviors—not feelings. There are many courses available to teach basic internet skills in 4-8 hours. You can buy a computer, assuming you have the money, in even less time. Learning takes practice and comfort is likely to come with greater skill—also requiring practice. But this does seem to be an attainable goal. You do want to set a realistic time period. This is doable in one year—but might be a stretch in one week—especially if you have lots of other time commitments. Perhaps, do one of them a month—buy the computer by the end of one month, complete the internet course by the end of the second month, but the Dream Weaver class might take 2-3 months to complete. Give yourself 6 months for all of it.

What action you take right away is completely in your control. You can go to the library or a book store and read about personal computers with the intent of deciding what kind of computer you want, you need, and can afford. Do it!

In order to sustain goal directed effort, we need feedback and rewards. Feedback keeps you working towards your goal, and provides you with information about whether you are on or off track. Your commitment to the goal increases when you have some reward to look forward to once you've reached your goal. The reward is only motivating for you if it is something you value.

6. So list ways you plan to get information, feedback, about how you're progressing towards your goal.

7. What reward do you intend to give yourself once you've achieved your goal? You might want a material reward, a social award, or even a self-congratulatory award. It is important that you really do celebrate your achievement and give yourself the reward. You wouldn't want to disappoint yourself or teach yourself that you are a liar, now would you? If you promise yourself an award, give it to yourself. And don't skimp. And don't get so busy with the next goal that you skip your rewards. If necessary as a reminder, write the reward down on the date you set to have your goal achieved.

Remember! You can do goal setting for other areas of your life using the same process. And the principles are similar when doing goal setting with others:

- brainstorm possibilities.

- prioritize them based on key values.

- discuss why they are motivating.

- select the ones you plan to attain.

- structure them as S.M.A.R.T. goals.

- list action steps to take. TAKE ACTION!

- decide how you will get and use feedback.

- decide on a team-based reward.

- celebrate your achievement together.

CHAOS SKILL DEVELOPMENT: *Storytelling*. One skill that can be useful in the Chaos leader's repertoire is the ability to manage the 'truths' and meaning in their organizations. Every leader is expected to be truthful if they wish to be trusted. But there are different kinds of truths that all leaders must contend with. Many of the more indirect Asian cultures teach us the subtleties of working with multiple truths, of multicolored meaning. Leaders can use stories to communicate both clear and complex messages about what is important in their organizations. Storytelling is an engaging, time-tested, and inexpensive way to communicate memorable messages. People like to hear stories. They learn from them and tend to share them with others, further reinforcing the message.

Typically, Chaos leaders are interested in a wide-range of subjects, bringing insights from unrelated areas to bear on problems in particular areas. They seek and share information, believing that information helps us all imagine possibilities never before considered seriously. They have to have some core sense of personal value and believe that they can actually solve the problems they encounter. They are often known to have a quirky sense of humor, to be playful, or at least not to take themselves (or others) too seriously—a characteristic that helps them maintain optimism and some sense of proportion in the face of what might otherwise seem to be overwhelming odds against doing-considering what they are addressing. They are willing to 'put up a balloon and see if it floats'—experimenting with ideas and not taking failures so seriously that they cease to try. They tell themselves and their followers a story that says 'we can do it' and get out there showing the way—failing, laughing, dusting themselves off when they fall, and trying again. For many Chaos leaders, not trying is the biggest failure.

One of the poems I learned by heart in the sixth grade captures the energy of the person who resonates to the Chaos style.

Somebody said it couldn't be done, but he with a chuckle replied,
maybe it couldn't but he wouldn't be one to say so 'til he tried.
So he buckled right in with a trace of a grin on his face.
If he worried he hid it.
And he started to sing
as he tackled the thing
that couldn't be done and he did it.

—— By Edgar Guest

The most powerful story a leader can tell is a story that contains a message that the leader has internalized themselves. Even a story heard from someone else, or read in a book, is more powerful when the leader makes it clear that the story has been important to them. The best way to make a story your own is to think about your own experiences or the point you want to make, understand the meaning you took away from the story (perhaps even share your understanding), and relate the story to you and your follower's experience in the moment. Finally, tell the story in a natural way—in your own words. Toastmasters, storytelling conferences, and even listening to speeches from people you admire are all good ways to improve your storytelling skills.

LYRICAL SKILL DEVELOPMENT: *Emotional Intelligence.* Daniel Goleman who is well known for bringing the idea of emotional intelligence to our attention, is very clear about what emotional intelligence is not. Emotional intelligence is not about being nice all the time. It is about being honest. Emotional intelligence is not about being touchy-feeling. It is about being aware of feelings, yours and others'. And emotional intelligence is not about being emotional. It is about being smart with your emotions. It is knowing how to use your passions to motivate yourself and others. And it is knowing how to keep your distressing emotions under control. Emotional intelligence, as defined by the original pioneers in the field, John Mayer and Peter Salovey, is a type of social intelligence that involves the ability to monitor our own and others' emotions, to discriminate among them, and to use that information to guide our thinking and actions. Or, more simply, emotional intelligence is knowing how we and others feel, why we feel that way, and what can be done about it. It is learning the difference between "I think" and "I feel", and hearing the difference when other people say that. And in this framework, emotions are neither good nor bad; emotions are information, valuable information.

There are five competencies associated with emotional intelligence:

1. Self-Awareness
2. Self-Regulation
3. Self-Motivation
4. Empathy
5. Effective Relationship Management

Self-Awareness is the cornerstone, the foundation that supports all of the other emotional intelligence competencies. The more we know about ourselves, the better we are able to control and choose what kinds of behaviors we will display in a work setting. Without self-awareness, our emotions can blind us and guide us to do things or to become people we really do not want to be. We must be at least aware of our thoughts and feelings in order to choose how we will respond to a person, situation, or event.

Self-Regulation is about recognizing our emotions and moderating our responses so that we are able to reason well. When we are angry, we cannot make good decisions, and often react inappropriately by blowing an event out of proportion. We lose perspective. Conversely, managing our emotionality assists us in communicating more constructively. Each of us can choose how to respond to and reframe emotion in ways that help rather than hinder our effectiveness in life. It is helpful to be able to recognize and learn to manage our own emotional triggers.

Self-Motivation. Once we are aware of how we feel and are able to manage those feelings, we can then direct the power of our emotions towards a purpose that motivates and inspires us. This ability to be emotionally behind ourselves, behind our purpose, gives meaning to our work and to our lives. Even the mundane is bearable with meaning. When people are intrinsically motivated, motivated from within, they accept change better, are more flexible, have better attitudes, take more initiative and do balanced risk taking. But most of all, self-motivation enables us to persist towards goals even in the face of obstacles and setbacks. Recognizing when and what emotions affect your performance—both propel you forward towards goals or depress/distract you away from your goals—is very important.

Empathy is learning to see things from another person's perspective so that we can relate to them better. Once we have become more honest and intentional with our own emotions, we can interact responsibly with others. We can now recognize and respond appropriately to the emotions of others with healthy boundaries about who is responsible for what feelings. Empathy has been associated with effective leadership in the research.

Effective relationships are the result of mastering the four competencies above—self-awareness, self-regulation, self-motivation and empathy. They are the stepping stones in the path of effective relationships. These competencies make us 'socially intelligent' rather than 'socially impaired'. The intent and impact of effective relationships is committed performance in organizations, more innovation, and more collaboration. These three create a cycle of effectiveness that then supports the development of these competencies for everyone in contact with them. Goleman and his colleagues run workshops and have written many books that provide additional suggestions for developing your EQ, your emotional intelligence.

STILLNESS SKILL DEVELOPMENT: *Challenging dis-empowering beliefs*. Most of us have times when we feel disempowered because the world, other people, or ourselves are not the way we think they should be. We replay our 'shoulds' and 'oughts' tapes in our minds so often that we feel powerless to manage our lives. Our negative judgments about others and/or ourselves make us miserable. Byron Katie teaches something she calls the Work. She has observed that despite the fact that we are told all the time not to judge, judging is what we do. So rather than fight reality, asking us not to do something we constantly do, she suggests we *judge our neighbors, write it down, ask four questions and turn them around.* To really do the work I suggest you first listen to a live session with Byron Katie, her C/D called *Loving What Is*, and/or visit her website at www.thework.org. Then, if you really want to know the truth, follow the instructions for doing the work provided here.

PART A: Choose a situation, past or present that feels unresolved in your life. Fill in the blanks about that situation with the questions below. Write out what stresses you in the form of a simple statement. Do not write about yourself yet. Be judgmental, uncensored and petty. Please do not be spiritual or kind. We have been instructed for years not to judge and it is still what we do best. Have fun! Give your problem the opportunity to express itself on paper. Remember to write short, simple sentences. Please write your answers. Do not do this in your head. It will not work as well.

1. Who or what don't you like? Who or what irritates you? Who or what saddens or disappoints you? *I don't like or I am angry at, confused, saddened, etc. by (name)............ Because..............*

2. How do you want them to change? What to you want them to do? *I want (name) .... To ....*

3. What is it that they should or shouldn't do, be, think, or feel? What advice can you offer? *Name .... Should or shouldn't ....*

4. Do you need anything from them? What do they need to give you or do for you for you to be happy? *I need (name) .... To ....*

5. What do you think of them? Make a list. *(Name)* .... *is*
    ....

6. What is it that you don't want to experience with that person,
    thing or situation again? *I don't ever want to or I refuse to*
    ....

PART B: It usually makes your judgments clearer if you
convert the statement after "because" to a "should" statement. For
now, leave off the feelings at the beginning of #1 but we'll return
to them with question three in the inquiry process. So if you had
written *"I'm angry and disappointed with Paul because he doesn't
understand me"* it would become *"Paul should understand me"* as
the beginning statement for our inquiry. Now investigate the
statement you wrote from the should form using the Work process.
Ask each of the Four Questions below about the statement. As an
example, we'll continue with the statement *"Paul should
understand me."* When doing your own work it is very important
that you let your mind ask each question, but listen for your answer
from your heart. Slow down and really listen. Contemplate.
Allow the response to surface from within.

The Four Questions are:
*   One: Is it true?
*   Two: Can I really know that it is true?
*   Three: How do I react when I attach to that thought?
*   Four: Who, what, or how would I be without this thought?

One: Is it true?   Perhaps, when you slow down you'll notice
that you feel-think that way about the person sometimes but not all
the time. Maybe it's partially true. You may even believe at this
point that your statement is absolutely true. So you investigate the
statement. Keeping with our example *"Paul should understand
me"* ask the question *"Is it true?"* You listen to your heart answer
and you say, *"Yes, it's true. Paul should understand me."* Or
maybe you'd say *"Sometimes Paul should understand me."*

115

Two: Can I really know that it is true? This question invites you to think more carefully about whether you really know it is true that Paul should understand you (continuing with our example). If it is really true that Paul should understand you and he doesn't understand you, at least not all of the time, then you are not looking at the reality of the situation. Does he understand you? Can you really know what is best for him or you? Can you really know that statement is true *"Paul **should** understand me."* If the reality is that he doesn't understand you (at least not all of the time) you will start to notice that some of your unhappiness might be do to your own belief that he *should* understand you, and he doesn't.

Three: How do I react when I attach to that thought? How do I treat myself? How do I treat others? (Especially the person I just judged). How does that feel? The question is really *"How do I react when I attach to the thought 'Paul should understand me"* *and then I know from question two that the reality is that he doesn't?* What is the effect? (Make a list of all the reactions you have—your thoughts, your feelings, and your actions—about yourself and about Paul). You might write down *"When I think* *"Paul should understand me" and he doesn't, I become angry and tense; I cry... How do I treat myself? I feel evil. I hate myself... How do I treat Paul? I hate him. I give him 'the look'. I try to change him. I don't speak to him...* (Picture him as you react in this way. What do you see?). As you investigate your thoughts in question three you can ask yourself *"Do I see a reason to drop this thought?"* (Please do not try to drop it.) Given all those negative results from attaching to the thought *"Paul should understand me"* and knowing he doesn't, it seems there might be some good reasons to drop that thought. But don't try to drop it. You're just investigating your thoughts and their impact on your life experience. *"Can I find one reason that is not stressful to keep this thought?"* (Be still as you experience your own wisdom.) Most people eventually answer this question with a *"No."*

<u>Four: Who, what, or how would I be without this thought?</u> (Picture yourself in the presence of the 'perceived enemy', the one who should understand you. Now imagine looking at that person, just for a moment, without the thought, *"he should understand me."* Watch. What do you see?) Until you see that person as a friend, even when he does not appear to understand you, your work is not done. Many times this is the beginning of release from the negative experiences that come with attachment to the judgment. You may start to feel lighter, to notice that you feel more kind towards Paul, happier with your self, or more open to relating to Paul.

PART C: The Turn-Around. Now turn around the 'should statement' you had from first step. For example: *"Paul should understand me"* becomes *"I should understand me"* and *"I should understand Paul"*. At times you may experience several turn-arounds, all of them as true or truer than the one you wrote from #1. Make amends to yourself and make amends to the one you have been blaming and attempting to change. It's often interesting to notice if you could or would do what you are expecting others to do. Be honest but easy with yourself. You are only doing this for your own peace of mind. Notice how you begin to get angry or stressed each time you think you want others to do what you think is best. And if you need to, go back to the four questions, especially question four: who would you be without the thought about how the other should be?

PART D: Continued inquiry. If you had other judgments from Part A, #1, investigate those using the four questions and turn them around.

Use the same inquiry procedure—questions one, two, three and four to write your answers to #2 from part A. Write the turnarounds. The do #3, and so forth. If you come up with more should statements along the way, use the four questions on those statements too.

PART E: Number Six. The turn-around for written statement #6 is *"I am willing to ..."* and then *"I look forward to..."*. For example: *"I don't ever want to experience an argument with Paul again,"* turns around to *"I am willing to experience an argument with Paul again,"* and *"I look forward to experiencing an argument with Paul again."* Each time you think you don't want to experience the anger or stress again, be willing to look forward to it. Number six is about embracing all of mind and all of life. Should the same thing happen again, give yourself a break—be gentle with yourself—and then do The Work again. Until all the hate and irritation dissipates, your work is not done.

It is best to do the Work in the beginning using surface judgments you have about other people. With greater skill using this inquiry process, the work provides a way to release yourself from painful thoughts about yourself, to unravel beliefs and scripts that have intense emotional content from your past, to make peace with some of life's most difficult challenges—illness, war, death, oppression, etc. There's no need to go searching for 'should thoughts' to investigate. We have them all the time. Start with the ones that present themselves. Our belief systems are interwoven such that as we start to unravel even surface beliefs we loosen them enough so that with patient inquiry we can unravel them all eventually.

THE SITUATION

Situation Matters. Sometimes, the situation actually calls forth aspects of an individual's character and supports that person as 'leader' within that context. For example, a person may be seen and appreciated by other people for their ability to mediate conflicts. A conflict arises and people may then seek out that person to help in the resolution. This person's character and behavioral style meant others were willing to follow them in this situation—a situation with conflict requiring a mediator. The 'leader' did not seek a conflict situation, nor did they seek to lead. Their particular set of skills were literally 'called for' in this situation.

Sometimes the situation frames the behaviors that will make a leader successful, amplifying the benefits of some leader characteristics and perhaps diminishing the importance of others. A particular person may be very organized, clear, directive, goal focused, and bossy. In general, that set of personality characteristics generate ambivalence with others—some people appreciate the clarity and organization but most of the time people do not like to be ordered around. Yet, when a crisis arises, people around that organized-bossy person may notice that this 'leader' is able to move forward without doubt regarding what to do. That person can be effective as a leader in a crisis situation. Other people may be willing to follow them then even if they would not do so in other contexts. The same behaviors and style can be effective in some situations and less effective in others.

Style and Situation. From the example above, we can see that certain situations seem to be ripe for skills associated with certain styles. Leadership is often most needed in times of change—but there are different kinds of change.

When we have evolutionary change—change that is continuous, clear, and inexorable, or when there's interpersonal conflict the Flowing style can be effective. The Flowing style is adept at co-opting and bypassing resistance. The leader's job in such situations is to stay centered and on track, redirecting the energy flow into the most productive channels. Flowing leaders influence their followers through their commitment, concentration, and sense of enacted purpose. They are creative in the ways they bypass or co-opt resistance and stay grounded in that purpose.

Staccato resonates to crisis situations where people need direction, structure, goals and/or decisive, quick action. Resistance is met with equal or stronger counterforce. The Staccato leader's job is to command, control, coerce, motivate, set boundaries, clarify goals, protect and direct everyone's energy using whatever means are necessary to get the job done with minimum costs and casualties.

In times of ambiguity, chaos and confusion—revolutionary times where control is impossible, outcomes unpredictable and powerful forces clashing the Chaos leader is called. The leader's job will be to tear down old thought barriers, smash through resistance if necessary. These thought structures need to be abolished so new ones can be built. They may slice through complexity, a situational Gordian knot, with some elegant, simple, effective solution. Chaos leaders are known to creatively unite disparate people, ideas and activities in new ways. Sometimes the situation is so chaotic that the most the leader can do is surrender while giving heart to followers—encouraging them to believe they can and will survive the situation. The Chaos leader may then use their charisma, comedic skills, and compassion to soften follower's fears.

The Lyrical leader is often effective in situations where they want/need to exercise influence but do not have direct, obvious, or positional power to do it. In many of these situations the outcome is not known, and the goal may not be clear. The situation may call for a project that requires a lot of commitment, buy-in, creativity from everyone, and lots of hands-hearts-minds to get things done, but the final output is co-created through this collaborative process. The Lyrical leader's job is to keep everyone involved, informed and committed to the shared goals while responding / adapting to any unforeseen shifts in the situation.

Stillness leaders can be particularly effective when the situation calls for a change in deep values, or some shift in the individual or collective belief systems. Stillness leaders listen, bring light to the shadow, and allow an integration that unleashes transformational energy for change. The leader's job is to empower the followers by being the change they wish to see, serving as catalyst, witness, and example of this transformational potentiality.

REFERENCES

Clawson, J. G. & Doner, J. (1996). "Teaching Leadership Through Aikido." *The Journal of Management Education*, Vol. 20, No. 2; pp. 182-205. Sage Publications.

POEM: Edgar A. Guest: It Couldn't Be Done.
　　　Guest, E. A. (1914). *Breakfast Table Chat*. Detroit.

Goleman, D. (1995). *Emotional Intelligence: Why it can matter more than IQ.* Bantam.

Goleman, D. (1998). *Working With Emotional Intelligence.* Bantam.

Goleman, D. (1998). "What Makes a Leader?" *Harvard Business Review, Nov/Dec*, 93-102.

Katie, B, & Mitchell, S. (2002). *Loving What Is.* Three Rivers Press.

Chapter 9
LEADER-FOLLOWER RELATIONSHIP
Lessons from Partner Dancing

Once you understand your own leadership style, you can be more effective in your interpersonal exchanges with others. According to Jim Kouzes and Barry Posner, "Leadership is a reciprocal relationship between those who choose to lead and those who decide to follow." Leaders learn to lead through interactions with others—an idea that has strong resonance in partnered dancing.

Think about it. Leading and following connote a relationship. There are no leaders without followers. This seems such a truism it feels as if it's barely worth mentioning, and yet many aspiring leaders forget all about the people they will lead. Instead, they focus on how they, as leaders, can improve the organization and become more powerful as leaders. In so doing, however, they create a relationship between themselves and an impersonal, fictional entity. Commonly, such leaders fail to recognize that the organization consists of real people, human beings, who must be acknowledged as partners in the co-creation of organizational experience.

In any collective dance experience there are at least these three choices:

- Lead
- Follow
- Co-create

It is not always necessary to lead. It is just as important to know who and when to follow. There is power and grace in visibly following your subordinate. And in practice, much leader-follower behavior is co-created in successful partnerships and groups.

Keeping with the dance of leadership metaphor, for dancers the music is like the leadership situation. Music sets the stage, evokes certain rhythms, and the dancer is effective or not depending upon how they work with the music. The entire dance experience is something more than the dancer(s) or the music. Since we're talking about leadership, we will envision an experience that contains music-situation, dancers (in this chapter, two partnered dancers), and some experience that relates the dancers and the music—i.e. the actual dance experience. To be effective, that is for the dance to occur, for people involved to enjoy it, and for people to feel expressed—the dancers and the music can interact in many ways—although some ways will be seen as more effective than others. Dance is wonderful for helping us learn *how to choose* our response to the music-situation and developing a *repertoire of effective responses* we can execute once we have decided what we want to do. One way to think of intelligence is by defining it as the ability to recognize and choose an effective and appropriate response to a situation. Then being able to respond to subtle details, thematic patterns, and the overall feel of the music as well as signals from your partner, are your dancing skills.

For leaders, the situation is the contextual equivalent to the music for dancers. Situations vary, as we saw in the last chapter, and each situation evokes certain kinds of responses. The leader will be effective or not, depending upon how they work with the situation. Whether the entire experience is effective will depend upon the interaction of the leader, the follower(s), and the situation. Effective leaders intend and cause a significant difference to occur in producing some shared goal (output), in enjoying the process of working toward that goal (satisfaction), and in co-creating an experience where they all learn skills that make them able to respond effectively in future encounters (learning). Like the dancer, leaders must *choose* a response to the situation and use their leadership skills to respond to subtle details, thematic patterns, and the overall feel of the situation and handle information coming from their followers.

Yes, I know that some people *seem* to be "born" dancers, as some people seem to be born leaders. But the good news is that the skills associated with effective response to the people-situation dynamics—the dance of leadership—can also be taught and learned, especially when those skills build upon characteristics, traits, passions, and interests that are part of the core personality of the leader. In the next chapter, I will describe skills we learn for team leadership from tribal dance. In this chapter, I will describe skills we learn in partnered ballroom dancing that translate well as leadership skills we can all learn. They are:

- Creating and using the frame
- Channeling resistance
- Co-creating the dance
- Tuning in to the situation
- Trust, then release

THE FRAME

One of the first lessons in ballroom dance is the creation of the frame. The leader places one arm so it supports the follower's back and the partner pushes their back into that hand. The leader's other hand is raised to elbow height and pushed against the partner's matching hand in front. This arrangement creates a frame for the dancers. The space within the frame must be big enough so as not to hamper the movements of one's partner, yet small enough that both dancers move as a unit on the floor. The frame also must be sufficiently firm so that both dancers are aware of each other's movements and are secure when gliding together, yet loose enough so that their individual movements are unhampered.

What is hidden from most observers of ballroom dance is that the partners co-create the frame. The leader sets the size of the frame by the setting size of the arm space. The follower pushes their back into one of the leader's arms and pushes their hand against the leaders other hand, thereby assisting the leader in maintaining the frame's stability through resistance. Followers within a well-defined leader frame feel a security that is liberating. They can trust that when they make a move that takes them slightly off center and/or out of their personal comfort zone, their leader will be there to provide some support and guide them back to center. It's great as a follower to know that your leader has "got your back." The follower can modify their pressure in order provide the leader with feedback, information that says 'watch out' or 'too much too fast'. The follower's pressure against the leader's hands makes it easy for the leader to give the follower signals about which direction to take. Without that pressure, it is more difficult for the leader to communicate efficiently with the follower. The frame is therefore a dynamic structure that facilitates leader-follower communication and movement. So in what ways does this metaphor apply to leading and following in every day life?

The leader's job. First, the leader's job is to provide the frame. The frame, in this metaphor, represents boundaries. The leader's job is to provide and manage the boundaries—physical, emotional, corporate, procedural, and structural—so that followers can do their work with support. Second, the leader must give clear, consistent, timely directions so that the followers can successfully do what needs to be done for both parties to achieve their joint goal. The directions must be communicated in a way that the follower understands or problems will ensue. This is directly applicable to leading in everyday life.

The follower's job. A follower's job is to give the leader feedback about their directing in a way that does not cause the leader harm. It does not help the partnership if the follower deliberately upstages or embarrasses the leader. Follower feedback to the leader is most effective when given with grace and subtlety, allowing the leader to adjust smoothly. Subordination of follower ego serves the partnership, but doesn't mean subservience to the leader. The follower needs to wait and respond to leader directions. It helps when the follower recognizes that the leader is also a follower, responding to the circumstances and feedback in the moment.

RE-FRAMING RESISTANCE

In everyday leader-follower relations, many people think of follower resistance as a problem. The ballroom dance experience, however, can help us reframe our ideas about resistance. In this dance, follower resistance is an essential element of the relationship between leaders and followers. Resistance makes it easier for the leader to support and guide the follower's movements. Without resistance there is no trust, no support, and movement becomes more erratic or ineffective. The resistance is leveraged for turns—turns being a metaphor for change in our model. Without follower resistance, leader-follower communication is less effective and the leader must work harder to signal changes in direction. On the other hand, if the follower does not give resistance, the follower loses the chance to *feel* supported by their leader, even when the leader wants to support the follower. Without follower resistance, the entire dance of leadership is less effective.

Resistance: the lever for change. In ballroom dance, the leader uses follower resistance to leverage turns. Making turns in dance is a metaphor for change. Remember! Leaders are often involved in change situations. In order to turn a partner efficiently, the leader in dance first pulls or pushes the follower in a desired direction. Push and pull can be thought of as two basic influence styles for leading—push (advocating, asserting, coercing) and pull (involving, empathizing, listening, asking open-ended questions). Leaders use push or pull to signal followers to change direction, and both turn cues can be effective in dance or leading, depending upon the change required.

After the push/pull, the leader loosens their grip so that the partner can turn as directed. The leader then raises their arm higher than the head of the follower or releases the hands so that the follower can make the turn without ducking. The follower makes the turn more easily when they have had some degree of resistance before the turn and as the turn is signaled, but not during the turn itself. For the pair to look good, neither partner ducks. Resistance, after the change has started, is not leveraged.

A leader who tries to push-turn a follower who is still in firm resistance is likely to *crank* the follower, something that's avoided in dancing for two reasons: it looks awkward because it takes both leader and follower off center (and in dance, if it does not look good, we don't do it) and it is likely to hurt the follower. Hurting a partner makes it less likely that you will work effectively together, now or in the future. Leaders who continue to crank followers, pushing too hard and too fast through strong resistance, past followers' limits, will diminish the latter's willingness to work with them. Therefore, both the type and timing of the influence style must work with the follower resistance in order to execute a smooth turn.

It is the follower's job to provide resistance, but not to be too rigid. A rigid follower makes it more likely they will be cranked—again not effective for the partnership. For the leader, follower resistance is the lever for change. Paradoxically, leaders can make the change occur with less effort when their followers resist. Even though this resistance may take many forms and occur for many reasons, it is effective for leaders to understand why the resistance is there and work with it. It is important for leaders and followers to remember that effective resistance typically precedes the agreement to and commencement of the actual turn-change.

Leaders must artfully decide when-how to push or pull followers along, and to distinguish when the members are resisting because they are not yet ready from when they are rigid. Sometimes, followers may need to change anyway, and the leader will be effective if they push. Sometimes the followers will need to change—and we saw some leadership approaches in the earlier chapters that can be effective in helping followers change. And occasionally, followers or leaders will need to be exchanged because there is not likely to be an effective partnership between that leader and those followers.

Communication: Using responsive contact. When people first start ballroom dance, it is not uncommon for the follower to provide the leader with what we call 'limp noodle' energy—that is, they place their hands where they are told to place them without any resistance, and they do not push their backs into the leader's palm that's resting on their back. When a follower is giving a leader no resistance, this is equivalent to complete follower compliance to any direction provided by the leader. Unfortunately, the leader has to think of what to do and provide enough energy to move themselves and to move their follower. The dance leader might also have to resort to giving a verbal direction, trying to explain or cajole the partner to take each step in particular directions. This can work, but it is a slow, cumbersome, inelegant dance—one that would not be much fun for leader, follower or audience. The follower is communicating to the leader, "I'll do whatever you want but I won't put any of my own energy into it."

The two of you may move around the room but the experience of this directed compliance is usually not very satisfying as a dance. Similarly, when followers merely follow leader instructions to the letter without providing any of their own energy or motivation, work gets done but it's usually far less satisfying. In our model of effectiveness, output without satisfaction is not effective long term.

We can also have the opposite—the follower who provides so much resistance that even though the leader is trying to give directions, no movement takes place because the follower is so rigid. Obviously then, there is no dance. It's as if the follower is saying to the leader "I'm not moving unless you can make me". Some leaders rise to this challenge and we end up with coerced movement. The follower will comply, often reluctantly. We have these situations in our every day experiences too—leaders who shove, coerce, control, dominate their followers in order to get them to comply with directives. The followers move and do what they are told, but only that. Again, this is not a satisfying experience for most of us.

I'm making stark contrasts here in order to make some potential lessons more clear. Sometimes we can cajole folks, get them started, and then they pick up steam and do the dance with us. Sometimes we control and coerce because that's all we have time to do and we need to deal with resistance quickly and forcefully so things get done. And I've described situations in earlier chapters where compliance or control could work. But when we need creativity and we want long-term effective performance towards a shared goal, commitment from both leaders and followers works better than either compliance or control. What communicates commitment in partner dance? Appropriate resistance from the follower, and caring direction from the leader: what I call responsive contact.

Follow with energy. Because leading is seen as desirable in our culture and following less so, many people think they should always lead—even if it's just leading themselves. We have constructed the notion that following is second best to leading, that doing it your way is better than collaborating, that you are either in charge or you submit. We would often rather do it alone than to submit to anyone else. And, what's really weird is, we really want our leaders to do it all, do it right, and provide perfect support even if we didn't ask for it and won't allow it. As a result, many people miss opportunities to follow effectively or to lean into support from their leaders because they do not understand the potential and need for resistance as followers. They flip flop between rigidity and wet-noodle-ish compliance. Appropriate resistance in the follower role is a sign of commitment—you are providing energy and information that can make the leader's job easier and your joint performance more effective.

I work with a lot of highly motivated, talented leaders as an executive coach. Because the most popular leadership model out there is one where the leader is out front, on top, and alone exhorting followers to follow them, these people often have never really allowed themselves to lean into the follower role. They want to be the perfect leader and follow the perfect leader. If they provide energy in the leader-follower relationship, they often think that it makes them the leader. If they are the follower, then they feel they should do what they are told or resist. It is often a huge insight for them to actually notice that there are people in their relationship network who would support them—have their back—if they would put some energy into the relationship, if they communicated commitment, provided information and gave real feedback to their leaders. In short, by using resistance constructively and leaning into their leader's support without rigid expectations of perfection, they might feel the support they assumed they did not have. Paradoxically, by being a good follower they gain even more support for their leadership.

CO-CREATING THE DANCE

In ballroom dancing, it is often clear who is the leader and who is the follower. In life, however, we are often simultaneously leaders and followers in dynamic relationships where we shift from one role into the other. But again to borrow from a kind of partnered dance, Argentine tango, men often practice with other men, and women with other women, before either dance publicly with the opposite sex. In this way, they each learn something about both leading and following in the partnered dance. Similarly, it is helpful for leaders and followers to experience each other's roles in order to understand the impact of their behaviors on one another.

In one of my leadership development programs we have a session entitled "Physical Metaphors for Leading and Following." Most of these leaders are surprised to learn how uncomfortable they are in the role of follower. Because they aspired to leadership early in life and successfully attained a leadership role, most of their attention has been on how they see things when thinking of themselves as leaders. They are sometimes surprised, when put into follower roles for the exercises, by how insensitive they might have been to their followers' needs and their own response-ability as leaders. It's one thing to read and talk about leading and following, it's another to actually experience it and debrief the meaning of that experience in real time. The insights learned from this session greatly enhance these leaders' willingness to respond differently to their followers' concerns when they return to their roles in their organizations. In our leadership programs, we spend a lot of time helping participants understand the power of allowing support from others, and that leaders and followers are always co-creating an interdependent dance.

The good news for leaders is that they are not expected to do it all. It's not their job to carry the people in their organizations. The good news for followers is that they can do more, better, with support and guidance from leaders without giving up appropriate resistance. Both leaders and followers must do their parts in their own space for the partnership to succeed. Both the leader and the follower are actually dancing to the tune of the situation and must maintain fairly close contact to maximize efficiency in communication. It makes both leader and follower look bad if the leader fails to lead well or the follower is unable or unwilling to follow.

TUNING IN: THE MUSIC-SITUATION AS MASTER

Dance also teaches us *to choose* our response to the music-situation and helps us develop a *repertoire of effective responses* we can execute once we have decided what we want to do. The dance skill repertoire includes: timing, appropriate response, knowing what to pay attention to and what to ignore, and responding with head and heart.

Timing. Dance teaches us about keeping pace with the music, being in sync with the beat, and moving with what is happening. Knowing when it is time to move, and even whether to move, is a variation on this issue. Some of the most interesting periods in the dance are the moments of stillness, contrasted with those of movement. Similarly, leaders often have some sense of when is the best time to respond in a particular way to a person or to a situation.

Appropriate degree of response. Some music will compel very subtle moves, like a soft flute calling forth a gentle sway. Other music, such as an insistent, throbbing drum, demands sharp accents. And there are many variations in between. However, intensity is not just loudness or extraversion; it is a quality felt on the subtler level by the energy harnessed and unleashed by the music. In each case, the dancer must provide the appropriate degree of response that matches the intensity of the music. The volume of the dance should match that of the music. Similarly, leaders' response volume or intensity should match their situation.

A leader must be able to distinguish an intense incident from a simply "loud" one.

Attention. Dancers know that each piece of music has many aspects one could attend to: the beat-rhythm, the melody, the speed, the different instruments, the overall feeling of the piece, the story the music/singer is telling, what is invoked in the dancer, and so on. Dancers may pay attention to any or all of these elements all the time or at different times as they interpret the music. Sometimes a leader needs to operate primarily at the superficial level, giving attention to detail and providing a competent, enjoyable, if slightly lighter dance. Sometimes leaders need to have their attention at the deep level—causing us to stop, think again, and move in directions different from what we imagined we could.

Head and heart. There was once an argument between two dance teachers, one exclaiming, "Technique! Technique! Technique! Technique is everything!" emphasizing the importance of the details needed to dance in any particular style. The other teacher responded, "Technique is nothing! Technique merely keeps your body from getting in the way of your expression!" pointing out that technique is not an end in itself, but merely a vehicle for expressing one's essence.

Yes, technique is important: it teaches us how to implement a movement, whether for dance or for leadership. Yet this technique vs. expression argument is a variation on the classic science vs. art debate heard in academia. Business professors tend towards management *science* (the head) with an emphasis on the importance of technique. They study, from an objective distance, what practitioners out in the business world are doing. Those engaged in management-organizational development practice outside the university setting, however, emphasize the leadership *arts* (the heart)—the importance of using the techniques available and necessary in the moment to effect the change we desire.

134

Dance is most beautiful when science and art are combined. Leaders are similarly most effective when they know how to do what must be done and then execute it artfully.

TRUST WHAT YOU KNOW, THEN LET GO

Dancing requires a combination of skill mastery and skill forgetting. One must surrender to the music, since, in the end, the music is the master. The music is in control. We all dance to the music—leaders and followers. The dancer does not control the music. We sometimes have this illusion, especially in these times of CDs and tapes. But even then, the music may skip or run at a slightly different speed.

Leaders in our presumed hyper-rational organizations still hold onto the illusion of controlling their situations. In Harvard Business School's MBA program, we even had a core course called "Control." MBAs continue to be taught that the manager's job is to control—especially change and complexity in their organizations. Many people form their own companies with the illusion that they will then be in control. Leaders are taught to command and control. Managers expend a lot of energy learning what to do when the music they've selected plays as expected. And that may work if things go as planned. But as we all know, most situations are not so simple. Unfortunately, by insisting on control, these managers may lose response-ability in face of increasingly rapid, ever present situational change. This book has been more about leading than managing. Leaders are often called in situations that are already dynamic, in the flux of change—or in situations that require change. Many times change cannot be controlled.

Sometimes the leader can be most effective by surrendering to something greater than the individuals involved. Surrender to meaningful purpose changes us all. A willingness to surrender the illusion of control can often be especially empowering for leaders in change contexts. Most obvious is the example using the chaos

135

rhythm. Chaos theory says that order can emerge from chaos. Chaos leaders can tolerate living without predictability, without over-controlling—allowing the energy to self-organize itself into shape, yes; but controlling it, no. They often find that there is more strength and resiliency in their organizations than ever imagined. Their ability to live with ambiguity is a source of power in our complex, unpredictable world.

Leadership is more about mastery than management. What do I mean by "master"? In the old days, people called dance teachers "masters." Dance masters were extremely accomplished performers as well as superior teachers. A true dance master does not teach others to be followers or mini-clones of themselves. Rather, they share themselves and their art, expecting that their students will become master teachers some day. Similarly, leaders encourage their followers to develop and exercise leadership. They focus on individuals and encourage them to be more themselves in the service of a goal. As Lao Tzu, the Chinese Master said 2500 years ago *"The wicked leader is s/he who the people despise, the good leader is s/he who the people revere, the great leader is s/he who the people say 'we did it ourselves'.*

We are all masters over what we pay attention to and how we frame its meaning. Deciding to relinquish our intentional control over others' performance, while trusting in our ability to respond effectively to what's happening in the moment, is a key lesson for leading. This is what I call *response-ability*. Rarely can we really control the situation or other people. We all dance to the music. Mastery lies, in part, in understanding this valuable lesson. We are not always in control AND we still have response-ability. We can still intend. We can still influence. We are wise masters when we understand and encourage others' mastery.

FOLLOWER-LEADER RECIPROCITY: LESSONS FROM CONFUCIUS

We return to Asian philosophy to explore insights into the leader-follower relationship using a mini-case based on the Analects of Confucius. Confucius was one of China's most famous philosophers and the founder of one of the most pervasive philosophical traditions in Asia. Like Sun Tzu (from the Art of War), Confucius was shaped and shared his view of life during the time of the warring states period in China, 2500 years ago. One might say Confucius and Sun Tzu offered contrasting prescriptions for how humans might interact effectively with each other. The Confucian philosophical tradition is humanistic, rational, and moralistic. Confucius taught that virtuous relationships founded on the individual pursuit of humanistic ideals, such as benevolence and goodness, could save society from the destruction to which it was otherwise headed. Confucius addressed specific relational roles and the reciprocal obligations of parties within those relationships; leader-lead, parent-child, husband-wife, elder-younger siblings, and friends.

Confucian ethical and political teachings were very important in Chinese teachings for over two thousand years. They also found receptive audiences in Korea and Japan. While Confucian ideology is rarely explicitly adhered to today, remnants of Confucian philosophy are evident in the many cultures which have had historical and cultural links to China, especially Asian values around the importance of family ties, hierarchy, propriety-saving face, and education.

Translations from Chinese characters into Western languages are particularly challenging. Every character in Chinese has multiple meanings. A few of the ones that were common in the Analects include:

"Way", translates the word "tao". This can mean "to lead", "road", "path", "way", "method", "art", "teaching", "to explain", and "to tell". It can also mean "the path of least resistance taken by water flowing downhill". Confucius refers frequently to the "way".

"Good" translates the word "jen". Other translations of "jen" include "benevolence," "humanity," "love," "altruism," "compassion," "kindness," and "co-humanity." Confucius seems to use the word "jen" to express the notion of virtue involving tenderness and accommodation to others, and as contrast to the more martial values described-prescribed by scholars such as Sun Tzu.

"Ritual" translates the word "li". "Li" might also mean "propriety," "ceremony," "decorum," "etiquette," and "manners." In the Analects, Confucius seems to use "li" to refer to a code of behavior evident in social relationships.

"Moral force" translates the word "Te", which may also mean "virtue," "power," "integrity," and "potency." "Te" seems to have both receptive and active connotations. In the receptive (or yin) sense it means the inner power of quality of being straight and true to one's essence. In a more active (or yang) sense, it means the power to arouse or communicate this inner power.

Each of these words is used to convey key concepts important in Confucian philosophy. Just exploring their complex meanings gives us some indication of the power of Confucian thought and practice.

Excerpts from the Analects of Confucius:

When asked "Is there one word which may serve as a rule of practice for all one's life?" Confucius said, "Is not Reciprocity such a word? What you do not want done to yourself, do not do to others."

When asked about perfect virtue. The Master (Confucius) said, "To be able to practice five things everywhere under heaven constitutes perfect virtue... Gravity, generosity of soul, sincerity, earnestness, and kindness. If you are grave, you will not be treated with disrespect. If you are generous, you will win all. If you are sincere, people will repose trust in you. If you are earnest, you will accomplish much. If you are kind, this will enable you to employ the services of others".

The Master said, "The way of the superior man is threefold, but I am not equal to it. Virtuous, he is free from anxieties; wise, he is free from perplexities; bold he is free from fear.

"When a prince's personal conduct is correct, his government is effective without the issuing of orders. If his personal conduct is not correct, he may issue orders, but they will not be followed.

"If people be led by laws, and uniformity sought to be given them by punishments, they will try to avoid the punishment, but have no sense of shame. If they be led by virtue, and uniformity sought to be given them by the rules of propriety, they will have the sense of shame, and moreover will become good".

When asked "What do you say to killing the unprincipled for the good of the principled?" Confucius said, "In carrying out your government, why should you use killing at all? Let your evinced desires be for what is good, and the people will be good."

Confucius taught a lot about communication in relationships. He asserted that words without action were wasted; that listening is as important as speaking, and that good communicators are not necessarily good leaders. *"The superior man (leader) wishes to be slow in his speech and earnest in his conduct."*

The Analects also refer frequently to the Arts, especially music and dance. Confucius seems to see the Arts as a manifestation of ritual, a means of achieving and experiencing harmony, and as evidence of 'te' in a leader. He asserted that the traditional arts teach inner balance and serve to develop a leader's moral constitution.

Confucius also notes that leaders for the future must recognize that they will be followers as well as leaders. In order to get things done, one person must lead; the other must follow. Effective followers, however, do not follow blindly. In fact, effective followers need similar skills to those required of effective leaders. Learning to be a good follower is an excellent way to learn to be a good leader. In order to succeed, one has to realize that being a leader or a follower is a role—not a personal trait.

REFERENCES

Kouzes, J. M. and Posner, B. Z. (1995). *The Leadership Challenge.* Jossey-Bass.

CASE: Confucius
    Legge, J., translator. (1971). *Confucian Analects, The Great Learning* and *The Doctrine of the Mean.* Dover Publications.
    "The Analects of Confucius." (1995). Leadership case from the Hartwick Humanities in Management Institute at Hartwick College. Oneonta, N.Y.

Chapter 10

TEAM LEADERSHIP
Lessons in Leading Teams from Tribal Dance

THE EMPOWERMENT A.C.T.:
AUTHORITY, COMPETENCE, TRUST

I have spent many years studying empowered work teams. In my research, people defined empowerment in practice as encompassing three criteria: authority, competence, and trust. High performing teams, like tribal dance troupes meet those three empowerment criteria AND have leaders who work with the team to support these criteria.

In the tribal style dance I do, the lead dancer will be slightly in front of the others. The leader then performs a series of steps to the music. With either no or very subtle non-verbal cues, the leader changes the steps. The dancers do not know exactly what steps the leader will do, nor do they know when. The process is improvisational. The leader and followers know all the steps, but the combinations are not choreographed. The music and its rhythm provide the context. The leading and following dancers have an agreement to do repetitive movements—in particular, the leader will repeat each movement enough times for the followers to be in sync. The repetition of shared movement repertoire means a co-created and structured process exists in the dance. The dancers who are following do not focus too tightly on the lead dancer's moves. Instead they use soft, peripheral focus, relax, and let their bodies move without trying to think about each movement or step. When this is done well, the following dancers pick up on change in the lead dancer's steps within a beat or two. Sometimes the followers change steps so smoothly with the leader that it seems as if they are reading the leader's mind or that the dance was choreographed. They're actually reading the leader's body, without the touch or directed signals inherent in partner dancing. It is hypnotic to watch this effect. In addition, as the group turns and moves around the space, the leader role shifts to a different person. Indeed, the roles of leader and follower flow with the dance and the music.

Each group member is able to decide what steps the group will do to the music when they are leading. Sometimes the entire group will do the same movements with one leader. Sometimes, within a dance, several leaders and followers will perform in sub-groups, or the large group may stay together but individuals will execute mini-solos using the group style. The leadership role shifts as the music changes by collective agreement of the group. This is a leader-_with_-follower relational dynamic rather than a leader-_over_-follower permanent positional dynamic.

Authority: Tribal dance is characterized by shared and shifting authority. The leader is not necessarily set for the entire dance. Different people can lead the dance at different times. And whoever is leading decides which steps to use from the shared repertoire. Similarly, with a team of competent people, it is possible for leadership to be shared among all team members. No one person needs to take responsibility for leading the entire project, for instance. Whoever is leading does have a responsibility to communicate to the followers, to select steps the entire group can perform well, and to repeat those steps often enough to that the tribe is in sync. In your team, if you have decision-making authority for some aspect of the team tasks, you too need to be responsive to the capabilities and concerns of your team members, and keep everyone focused on the team goal. In a tribal dance troupe, we want the entire troupe to perform well and enjoy the dance—and we want our audience to enjoy it too. In your team, you want to make sure everyone performs well, enjoys working together, and you get the job done to the satisfaction of whoever has to use your team's output.

Competence: In tribal dance, the degree of skill required of each individual can be less than what is required of soloists, AND you can still get a complex, beautiful dance. How is this possible? The complexity comes from the individuals' variety of movements, weaving a textured tapestry composed of simple moves (when any individual is followed like a single strand). However, when combined with each of the other dancers and the music, the picture that emerges is strikingly complex.

We can also work well with diversity within the group context better than within partnered dancing. The group effort can highlight and support the unique expression of each person's solo abilities. The key is to position each individual so that the group is able to make maximum use of his or her strengths while it supports (that is, makes less visible) his or her weaknesses. In this way, the pressure on each person is reduced. There is not as much demand to get every move right, as there would be in solo or partner dancing for a number of reasons:

- the moves can be simpler for each dancer,
- the soloist can dance for less time,
- the soloist feels the support of the group while doing 'their thing' in the spotlight,
- the person most comfortable and skilled with a complex move undertakes it out front while the others shift position based on their comfort and confidence performing that move.

Each member of the troupe, like each member of a team, still needs to know how to execute her or his steps properly with the correct timing. Group members rely on each other to do their part. As each one performs, the entire group seems to pulse in collective agreement. Individual style and goals are subordinate to the group's style. Empowered teams, like tribal dance troupes, must balance individual expression against group norms and goals. Team leaders must be careful not to define the group norms/goals so tightly that individual expression is squeezed out, and the group descends to the lowest common skill level.

Trust. One of the ways that followers are able to match their movements to the leader's movements so quickly is that all group members are taught to shift from focal to peripheral vision. The intent is to move the individual from that sense of self, as separate from but following the leader, to a place where the brainstem takes over. There is no conscious thought. The eye sees and muscles respond to what is in the visual field without going through higher cognitive processing or choice. This is trusting the leader, trusting the group, trusting the body. It is seeing movement that is so rapid there is little time lag between the leader shift and the group response. High team trust is what most differentiates high performing real teams for so-so performing nominal groups. That trust is a sink-or-swim-together bond that causes group synergy—a dynamic process of co-creating more than the sum of the individual parts.

HIGH PERFORMING TEAMS

So what are some lessons for leading empowered teams to be derived from tribal dance? Because each member of the group knows the purpose and is skilled *enough* to lead and follow, anyone at any time can lead or follow. Authority is shared. Each member of the team needs to be good enough at their job to contribute to the overall team goal, but does not have to be an individual superstar to make a contribution. For those skills where they do excel, they contribute significantly to the team, and as each person contributes the truly excellent skills, but is supported by teammates when they are less skilled, the overall net result is synergistic. And they all have more fun and less stress in the process. No one person has to carry the weight of overall team success or failure. Teams are best used in situations where you have complex, interdependent tasks that require everyone's contribution to succeed. By definition then, we can capitalize best on team member's expertise by not expecting any one person to do every thing well or do it all alone. Members also trust each other and the process, understanding that it does not diminish the individual to be at one with the group for a particular situation.

In work, my best experience with empowered team work was when I worked for a company that provided high quality customer service training. I could sense the alignment in purpose when I first walked in the door for an interview. Everyone knew what the company did, that they did it well, and why they did it. Each person I interacted with was clear about and focused on their mission. My co-workers really believed we all needed to act in ways consistent with the training we provided other corporations. In fact, **every** employee had some say in whether or not to hire me: the receptionist, the mail clerk, the secretaries as well as the managers with whom I had scheduled interviews. The sense of connection to mission was palpable and positive. The organization had a positive force field, and even as an outsider, I felt drawn in, attracted to that force. This organizational energy occurred in part because everyone there was committed to making a significant difference. We all had decision-making authority appropriate for our respective roles as consultants, specialists, and managers AND we were all committed to helping our organization be a model of the quality customer service we taught others. Each person was different and we had a wide range of skills—but we shared the commitment to the creation of a quality product in a respectful climate for everyone.

Sometimes people will ask me how tribal dancing differs from something like an improvisational jazz group. In many improvisational jazz combos, each musician is given a certain amount of time to perform as a soloist. The musician will often demonstrate virtuosity with their instrument within this allotted timeframe. Then the next musician takes a turn. And then the next. As they each do their thing, I often feel that the cohering principle, the sense of a group groove is lost. I can appreciate each soloist as they do their thing but sometimes when the group cohesion is not there, the sum of the solo-after-solo experience feels competitive. If I were to apply the findings from my empowerment research, I would describe the improvisational jazz experience to be akin to empowered, co-acting individuals performing in their unique ways without a sense of group-team cohesion.

In the tribal dance style, the virtuosity of the dancer is seen in the ability to express their uniqueness *through* the group form. Individuality, contrary to many people's assumptions about this type of team activity, is not lost. For instance, when new members join my tribal dance classes or the tribal troupe, they learn the group repertoire and they are asked to come up with a combo that becomes their unique contribution to the troupe repertoire. Usually, they teach that combo to all of us, and lead that combo when we dance it, if they wish. We also name the combo after them, providing personal acknowledgement of their contribution. So the team experience is relational and collaborative but not de-individualizing. Individuals are invited to find value in giving up their personal points of style AND still sharing their uniqueness in the group. Each person's contribution makes that dance with that group work. In the end, the dances bear the mark of each person's contribution. So, tribal dance is structured improvisation with individual expression.

One of the easiest new skills to learn in leading empowered teams is to ask individuals about what contributions they'd like to make to the team, and to then acknowledge them personally when they make those contributions. Setting the norm, that every member is expected to contribute and will be acknowledged for doing so, greatly enhances participation in, motivation for and commitment to the team and its tasks. Next time you are in team meeting, try doing that (because in an empowered team any one can lead from their area of competence). For example, let's say you work with someone who is really good at developing graphical models to summarize complex data. This person has just designed and presented such a model at a team meeting—say a new model for reviewing risks & opportunities. Instead of just jumping in and building on their ideas, critiquing the model, or showing how it could be improved, slow down and say "I really like *Jackie's* model for looking at risks and opportunities. Let's use it when we prepare our report." I assure you that Jackie will be pleased to know someone noticed that effort. If you're lucky enough to have several people suggesting models—put each of their names next to their ideas. If almost every one has put something forth and you have one or two people who have not, ask them to suggest modifications to the model they like most and then rename it to include them both. The idea is to personalize recognition for contributions made to the team effort in such a way that you engage everyone on the team.

We are now expected to work in teams all the time. People will often ask me for examples of teams/groups in action—other than sports teams. I often refer to music and the arts. It is common for chamber orchestras or jazz combos to have to work out the same group dynamics and team leadership issues we think of more commonly in the office setting. In my mind, jazz combos are not always acting as 'real teams' but rather as collections of individuals—what we in social science call 'coacting' groups. In your organizations, a coacting group would be a collection of individuals who all report to the same boss, but who do their work separate from each other and who are all rewarded based on their individual performance. In contrast, tribal dance troupes seem to operate more as 'real' teams—coordinating their movements in order to create a group experience shared with their audience.

Using my research framework, I see the improvisational jazz experience as being more like empowered, co-acting individuals performing in their unique ways without a sense of group-team coherence. A chamber quartet, on the other hand, would have more shared structure in the music, less individual improvisation-authority to change the music, but be a tight real 'group' experience. I love solo jazz performance—when I expect solo jazz performance. Chamber quartets can also be fabulous, when that is what I expect. I happen to prefer something in between the individualized improvisation and not-quite-a-real-group feel of the jazz combo and the tight group experience with limited improvisation of the chamber quartet. When I'm performing and in my work, I do my best with structure and room for individual improvisation that serves the team experience.

What can be most jarring for me is to expect a coherent group performance and then experience a competing-individuals-pretending-to-be-a-group performance. You may have had that experience at work—you are supposed to be a team but you (and others) are not acting like a team, do not have team spirit, nor team goals, nor team rewards. Sometimes, people in organizations describe a similar experience when they watch senior leadership teams interacting without much regard for what is happening to or with their followers—the front line—or competing as department heads against each other. Many people feel one of the worst organizational experiences is this saying one thing (we are a team) and doing another (acting like individuals).

When it comes to "team" leadership, your first task is actually to make sure a team is what you need and want. Then you have to decide what kind of group-team you need—the more improvisational jazz combo, where you mostly coordinate the activities of highly skilled individual co-actors; the chamber quartet, where the team is tight but not that empowered to execute anything other than the instructions you-the-music-situation-structure allows them to do; or the tribal dance troupe, where empowered competent people collaborate and improvise in a co-designed structure. Your leadership tasks will differ depending on both degree of teamness you need and amount of authority, competence, and trust (empowerment) those team members have.

To be sure, there are times when you need to pull people together but give them directives. When? When you have very little response time, when you have no choice but to comply with laws, when you are in an emergency situation, when your team members are just getting together and don't know-trust each other yet, and when they are new to the job.

And, of course, there are times when you want to lead an empowered team—when? When you want-need a highly committed organization, when you need psychological buy-in from the people working with us, when you truly need each person's talents to get the organizational tasks done, when they are willing and able to work together as a team, and when they are all skilled enough to do what needs to be done. Many of us believe leaders are people of extraordinary ability who take on great tasks on behalf of something greater than themselves. Improvisational tribal dance suggests that there are many everyday leaders, people willing and able to make a positive difference in their organizations, if and, when those who desire solo status all the time would just turn, let go, and let someone else lead for a while. The whole group looks good, maybe even better, has more fun, and is more energized when this occurs. The dance of leadership is the art of knowing which situation calls for which kind of leadership.

REFERENCES

Johnson, R., & Thurston, E. K. (1997). "Achieving Empowerment using the Empowerment Strategy Grid." *Leadership and Organization Development Journal: vol:*18/2, pp. 64-73. MCB University Press.

Maznevski, M., & Johnson, R. (1997). "Empowering the Multicultural Team." *Business & the Contemporary World.* John Wiley & Sons.

Chapter 11
THE DANCE OF LEADERSHIP

Leaders-leadership is everywhere. Despite a limited media image of leaders and leadership, we find that leading as a term is omnipresent, and leadership as an activity is universal. We find leaders in every walk of life throughout time, in all races-creeds-colors-nationalities-genders, ages—everywhere.

Leadership is easy to recognize and challenging to do. Leadership is not necessarily any single act, though it can be. Yet leaders, to survive and continue to have influence, must adapt and diversify in ways that make it possible to continue to be effective with their followers in our ever-changing environments. And the quality of leadership depends very much on things leaders do not truly control such as context, timing and the perceptions of the led.

WE NEED YOU!

We need as many people as possible acting from positive intention. We have lots of problems that need attention. Our organizations, communities, and societies need both more leaders and different leaders. We need leaders who can influence lots of different kinds of people, especially given the changing demographics domestically and the shift to globalization generally. We also need committed, rather than coerced followers. We need

151

leaders who dance to all the rhythms because we've got all kinds of change going on—conflict, crisis and chaos requiring commitment, courage and creativity. Yes, Staccato and Chaos leadership styles work in crisis and chaos situations, but we need the other styles, too—Lyrical, Flowing, Stillness—that involve more people, encourage us, spur creativity, and garner commitment.

INNER RHYTHM – OUTER IMPACT

Effective dance movement comes neither from the head nor just the feet but from within—the center. Leading from within means leading from within your organization but also from within your self, your center, your core. You must give yourself permission to dance your own dance. The dance of leadership is an expressive art—it expresses you. When I dance, I'm doing the Robin Johnson dance. When you dance, you own your expression, your energy. Your authenticity and aliveness attracts others to you.

The irony lies in the fact that these lessons in leading are here, within you right now—not somewhere else, with some power figure who gives you permission to lead, or some guru whose wisdom you must tap. We often search for answers outside ourselves rather than gathering what is within us in the moment. Whatever you're doing in life, you have opportunities to lead. *Right where you are, do what you can! Look for the places where you can say: "Yes."*

There is a presumption when you join or start an organization that if you work hard, and you are ambitious, you'll become a leader. But if you don't reach the pinnacle called 'leader', by no means should you construe that as a sign of failure. Many people just like you are seeking self-validation. They want to know that their efforts having meaning, even if they never aspire to become head honcho. The *Dance of Leadership* conveys a validating message for people without "position" of every race, every age, and every culture who are still actively idealistic enough to believe their efforts can make a significant difference in the world.

Some of us think we'll finally be OK if we start and run our own business, thinking we'll finally get to do it our way. Many of the leadership books currently on the market target these top-of-the-pyramid readers. In truth, however, large groups of us—the majority, really—will never become CEOs. Some of us don't even want to. And even if you are the CEO—in this world you can't truly run a business or organization by yourself. Not being able to do it all by yourself makes it even more important to understand yourself as a leader.

Leading is more than position. Having formal leadership position with decision-making authority is both a resource and a constraint. On the one hand, it can bring access to systems and resources. On the other, formal authority carries a set of expectations—and often, unrealistic expectations, at that.

Leading from within—being outside the formal power structure but within an organization—can be an advantage. You can have more freedom of movement, the opportunity to focus on what you see as the issue (rather than the organization's or others' focus), and there is a stronger chance that you'll be in touch with what people in the trenches are really feeling. You have a greater opportunity for connection. It's not that I'm urging you to aim for the middle. Mediocrity is not the goal here. But I do ask that you aim for making a meaningful difference, whatever position you're in.

WHO ARE YOU? WHAT DO YOU WANT?

In life there are two questions: Who are you? And what do you want? Freud said we want to do meaningful work and to love. I believe that we want to love our work, and that makes it meaningful. In order to do our work well, we have to know who we are. Each of us is here with certain talents, interests, and

153

developmental paths that will contribute to the collective good. On a deeper, more spiritual level, ignoring, dismissing or failing to develop who we are is sacrilegious. All of the ways we limit ourselves, discount ourselves, doubt ourselves, have to go before we can dance the dance we are.

LEADING IS BELIEVING

In many ways "Leading is Believing." You need to understand yourself as a leader or else you won't lead. You need to be able to recognize situations that call for your skills so you will use those skills to make a positive difference in those situations. You need to believe it's possible to be authentic, to be real, and know that your authenticity is in itself going to make a difference. The *Dance of Leadership* is about leading from within—from within who you are at the core and also from within your organization. So remember! It's really up to you. Do you want to make a positive difference within your sphere of influence? Do you want to be your whole and true self while making that difference? Are you willing to relate authentically and responsibly to others?

Then what are you waiting for?

Let's work like we don't need money,
care like we'll never be hurt,
dance like no one's watching, and
give like it's heaven on earth!

ABOUT THE AUTHOR

Robin Denise Johnson, Ph.D.

*I dance
and the world
dissolves
into the
wholeness
it always was!*

D r. Johnson is a performing artist and teacher of fusion-style tribal dance. See www.tribalfusiondance.com. She has combined her love of dancing with her knowledge of teaching, leadership and group dynamics. She has taught and coached MBA's and executives in authentic leadership for over 25 years as a manager and educator. She currently provides consulting and training to corporate executives, managers, and educators through her company, EQUEST, Inc. See more at www.equestinc.com. Dr. Johnson is Associate Professor of Management and Human Resources at the College of Business, California State Polytechnic University, in Pomona. Dr. Johnson has been active as faculty director, co-designer and/or teacher in executive education programs at both the Anderson School of Business at UCLA and the Darden Business School at University of Virginia. Dr. Johnson earned a Ph.D. in Organizational Behavior from Harvard University with an award-winning dissertation on empowerment and diversity. She holds an M.A. in Social Psychology and earned first year honors from her MBA studies at Harvard Business School. She received a B.A. in International Relations and History from Brown University.